The Magic of
Christmas Miracles

ALSO BY JAMIE C. MILLER, LAURA LEWIS,
AND JENNIFER BASYE SANDER

Christmas Miracles:
Magical True Stories of Modern-Day Miracles

The Magic of Christmas Miracles

AN ALL-NEW COLLECTION OF INSPIRING TRUE STORIES

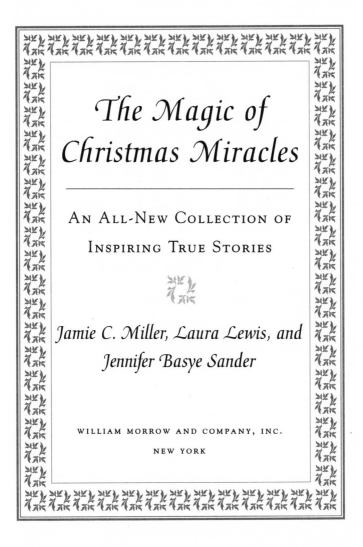

Jamie C. Miller, Laura Lewis, and Jennifer Basye Sander

WILLIAM MORROW AND COMPANY, INC.

NEW YORK

A Big City Books idea

It is the policy of William Morrow and Company, and its imprints and
affiliates, recognizing the importance of preserving what has been written, to
print the books we publish on acid-free paper, and we exert our best efforts
to that end.

Library of Congress Cataloging-in-Publication Data

The magic of Christmas miracles : an all-new collection of inspiring
true stories / [edited by] Jamie C. Miller, Laura Lewis, and
Jennifer Basye Sander.
p.   cm.
ISBN 0-688-16456-0
1. Miracles.   2. Religious biography.   3. Christmas—Miscellanea.
I. Miller, Jamie C.   II. Lewis, Laura, 1963–   .   III. Sander,
Jennifer Basye, 1958–   .
BT97.2.M33   1998
242'.335—dc21   98-23939
                                                                        CIP

Printed in the United States of America

First Edition

1   2   3   4   5   6   7   8   9   10

BOOK DESIGN BY JO ANNE METSCH

www.williammorrow.com

To Julian, Evan, Olivia, Alex, Ian, Kelly, Seth, and Ryan

For showing us the magic in everything

CONTENTS

Contents

Contents

INTRODUCTION

CHRISTMAS IS A magical time of year. The streets are draped with twinkling white lights that sparkle in the wet road below, soft strains of familiar carols accompany us wherever we go, and the warm smells of home-baked breads and cookies fill our houses with sweet anticipation.

As children, we, each and every one of us, believed in the magic of Christmas. We lay awake at night on Christmas Eve, straining to hear the tinkling sound of sleigh bells and the tapping of reindeer hooves. We believed. We stood next to the crèche and looked with awe at the tiny figure of the baby Jesus as He lay on the straw. We believed.

But as we grow older, it seems that no smell is as pungent, no music as poignant, no memories as dear as those from our childhood Christmases. As we rush from crowded mall to after-school pageant, staying up late at night struggling with toy-assembly instructions, wrapping paper, ribbon, and

Christmas cards—we wonder if we have perhaps lost something along the way. At some point in our hurry to cross every item off our list of things to *do* and things to *buy*, we suddenly become aware that those *things* don't matter nearly as much as we think they do when we're caught up in the race to get them done.

For a few brief moments in the midst of our holiday frenzy—if we're lucky—we catch our breath and get a glimpse of the real magic of Christmas. If we lift our eyes, we will recognize the light in the eyes of the people we pass, and if we look behind their faces to their hearts, we will see people hungry for comfort and love. At these moments, it is suddenly clear to us that it's not the decorations and the wrapping and the sleigh bells that matter at Christmastime; it's the people that matter. The warm, whole, happy feeling in our hearts comes as we witness small acts of kindness around us and as we ourselves give love and service to our families and to those in need.

Ask any child what he got last Christmas. Or the Christmas before. He might remember one special thing, but for the most part, the stacks of wrapped gifts are gone and mostly forgotten within a few weeks or months. Now ask any child to tell you what she remembers about the time she went caroling to a convalescent home or helped deliver a basket of Christmas goodies to a family in need. The warm feelings that accompany such experiences are not easily forgotten. Certainly, the receiving of gifts at Christmas is fun, but it is through the giving of self that the true magic of the season unfolds.

It has been said that "miracles are God's way of remaining

anonymous." But if God remains anonymous, the hands through which He works are clearly visible—the hands of common, everyday folks around us, performing quiet acts of kindness that turn sadness and tragedy into miraculous events, the healing of both body and soul.

And occasionally, those hands can even be our own. We all have the power to lift others and create miracles through simple acts of compassion—and we can never be sure just how far the effects of those acts will be felt. A small gesture can be like a stone thrown into the river of someone's life, the impact of the event rippling on and on. The only requirement is that we keep our hearts and minds open to the whispers that nudge us in the direction of others' needs.

We have collected thirty-three short stories in the hope that this Christmas season, you will be open to those feelings—and to the optimism, hope, and magic that were such a natural part of your childhood. Build a cozy fire, pour yourself some tea or hot chocolate, settle in on the sofa, and read true tales of miraculous and unexplained Christmastime events—a young girl in a coma who awakens upon hearing the sounds of her favorite song, "Angels Among Us"; a heartbroken woman who receives Christmas gifts from a kindly stranger on a bus; and a father whose inner emotions are finally touched by the sound of his own son's pure, sweet voice singing the songs of Christmas.

Similar stories struck a real chord with readers of our first book, *Christmas Miracles*. Many readers told us how much they enjoyed reading these stories aloud to their children, family, and friends. Some families told us they read one to their family each night between Thanksgiving and Christmas. And in a small way, the book caused its own miracle! While reading "The Town That Gave Christmas," a story about a needy family who receives ten crates of gifts delivered on Christmas Eve in the midst of a raging snowstorm, a family in Canada realized that they had been telling the same story for the past seventy years—but from the viewpoint of their grandfather, the postman who was inspired to make the difficult delivery.

We invite you to share your own stories of miracles with us. And not just Christmas miracles, but miracles of all kinds. If you'd like to share a story with us, just drop us a note. You don't have to write the story, but please be sure to include your telephone number so we can call you to hear the story. Write to the address on page 169.

We hope that the stories in this book will warm your heart and nourish your spirit. May they awaken in you the rich promise of small miracles in your own life, and add to the wonder of the season for your whole family.

—JAMIE
—LAURA
—JENNIFER

For an hour on Christmas Eve
And again on the Holy Day
Seek the magic of past time,
From this present turn away.

—ROBINSON JEFFERS
"Only an Hour"

The Magic of
Christmas Miracles

The Man
in the Muffler

WAS SIXTEEN WHEN my father left. That year there was no Christmas tree, no turkey dinner, no presents. My mother worked two jobs as a cleaning lady. I sold hats at a department store in downtown St. Paul, Minnesota. It was Christmas Eve, 1965. The store was closed. The streetlights were decorated with the tinsel of the season. Somewhere church bells tolled out "Silent Night." I stood alone on the corner and waited for the bus to take me home.

The wind whipped my thin coat and threatened to tear off my hand-knit hat. My mother had sewn a pair of corduroy pants to pull up under my dress, but I stubbornly carried them. It was better to freeze than look ridiculous.

It was a snowless December night, bitter and empty. I shivered against the wind and considered how one year had changed everything. My parents' marriage was over. My home and my heart were broken. The divorce did not surprise anyone but me. My father's fierce anger had exhausted my mother's forbearance years ago. But he had never gone away before, never abandoned us. It was because of him that there would be no family celebrations this year. I resented him for the destruction of my family. These were the things I thought as I lumbered onto the freezing-cold bus.

I found a seat next to the bus heater and placed my feet on the perfect spot. Hugging my corduroy pants, I cherished the small comfort of the heater as it eased the cold in the bus.

That is when it happened.

A man, perhaps in his sixties, appeared from somewhere in the back of the bus. He smelled of English Leather and Pepsodent, and wore a hat like Frank Sinatra used to wear. A fine Pendleton wool muffler hid half his face and he held a large shopping bag.

"May I?" he asked as he prepared to sit.

I looked away. I didn't speak to strangers, especially men.

He sat next to me and placed the shopping bag between us. I noticed the bus driver watching him in the mirror. Everything would be all right, I told myself. This man won't get away with anything. He sat beside me, studying my worn coat, my desperate hug of my corduroy pants. Bus heat rushed through the soles of my shoes, and I closed my eyes, allowing the warmth to help me forget him. Then he cleared his throat and touched my arm. "Excuse me," he said, "and pardon me for intruding. But I couldn't help notice that you are shivering. Are you all right?"

He peeked at me from behind his muffler and when his eyes met mine I saw something I had never seen before. It was the face of a kind man. For a moment, I felt the chill of the bus dissipate.

"You look tired," he said. "Have you had a tough day?"

When he spoke I realized that I was watching his concern for me take form. The sensation was new, foreign. My father's face was never filled with worry for me or anyone else. Anger, frustration, and fear were the foundation of his personality. Perhaps being a father made some men anxious and burdened. I wondered if this man had children. The bus made a gassy sound as it stopped, and he rose to leave. He held onto the handrail of the seat before him, and looked down at me for the last time.

"I get off here," he said. " I hope the rest of your Christmas is better than tonight."

I looked into his eyes and felt my throat tighten. For a moment I wanted to take his hand, to hold fast to this rare concern for me.

"Thank you, sir," I said. I heard my voice break.

He was nearly off the bus when I realized he had left his package.

"Hey, mister!" I called. He turned as the bus doors opened. "You forgot your things." I pointed to the bag.

"No I didn't." He pulled his muffler over his face again and waved. "You keep it." The bus doors closed behind him and he was gone. The bus driver insisted that I carry the package home, so I did. The house was dark when I arrived. My mother was sitting in the living room, asleep in her chair. At first she didn't believe me when I told her what happened, but my story was so marvelous that she came to accept it.

We opened the shopping bag and found three packages wrapped with red ribbon and golden paper. There was a box of Fanny Farmer white chocolate in one bundle, a bright red wool scarf in another. The smallest package held a tiny mother-of-pearl music box.

My mother wrapped the scarf around her shoulders and marveled at the large almonds in the white candy. "Maybe things will work out for us after all," she said. She handed me the music box. The tune it played was "Have Yourself a Merry Little Christmas."

When I lifted the lid, its song reminded me that there was one kind man in the world. If there was one, I thought, there must be others. If there are others, the world is not an ugly place and the lyrics to the song are true.

"Next year all our troubles will be miles away."

I treasure my music box still. It holds a gold ring from my husband, an old cameo from my mother, and the memory of a Christmas miracle.

—KRISTINE M. HOLMGREN
Northfield, Minnesota

A Father's Tears

NE AFTERNOON ABOUT a week before Christmas, shortly after my family of four piled into our minivan to run a short errand, this question came from a small voice in the backseat: "Dad," said my five-year-old son, Patrick, "how come I've never seen you cry?"

Just like that. No warning. One minute it's "Mom, what's for supper?" The next it's "Dad, how come . . ." My wife, Catherine, was as surprised by Patrick's question as I. But she is one of those lucky souls for whom tears come naturally, are spilled spontaneously, and then are quickly forgotten. Patrick has seen his mother cry dozens of times. So my wife was entitled to turn to me with a mischievous smile that said, Explain this one, Dad.

I couldn't, of course. I mumbled something in reply about crying when my son was not around, at sad movies, and so forth. But I knew immediately that Patrick had put his young finger on the largest obstacle to my own peace and contentment, the dragon-filled moat separating me from the fullest human expression of joy, sadness, anger, and disappointment. Simply put, I could not cry.

I know I am scarcely the only man for whom this is true. In fact, I believe that tearless men are the rule in our society, not the exception. When, for instance, did John Wayne shed tears, or Kirk Douglas, or any of those other Hollywood archetypes of manliness? In one movie that I recall, when Wayne's best buddy is slain on the battlefield, the Duke looks down to the body of his fallen friend with studied sobriety, but also with his typical calm. Then he moves on to the next battle with his typical bravado.

Passing centuries have conditioned us men to believe that stoicism is the embodiment of strength and that unfettered emotion is weakness. We have feigned imperviousness to the inevitable slings and arrows, traveling through life with stiff upper lips, calm on the outside, secretly dying within.

A recent television news report only confirmed what I have long suspected. According to the news, the number of men being diagnosed with depression today has skyrocketed. But I submit that we men have always been depressed to one degree or another, though we tend to medicate it with alcohol, or work, or afternoons and evenings sitting mindlessly in front of one television sports event or another.

Take me, for instance. For most of my adult life, I have battled chronic depression, an awful and insidious disorder that saps life of its color and meaning, and too often leads to self-destruction. Doctors have told me that much of my problem is physiological, an inherited chemical imbalance, something akin to diabetes. Those physicians have treated it as such, with medication.

But I also know that much of my illness is attributable to years of swallowing my rage, my sadness, and even my joy. Strange as it seems, in this world where macho is everything, drunkenness and depression are safer ways for men like me to deal with feelings than tears.

In my own battle, I had begun to see the folly of this long ago, well before my son's penetrating backseat query. I could only hope that the same debilitating handicap would not be passed on to the generation that followed mine.

Hence our brief conversation on a sunny December afternoon the day after Patrick posed his question. He and I were back in the van after playing together at the park near our home. Before pulling out, I turned to my son and thanked him for his curiosity of the day before. Tears were a very good thing for boys and girls alike, I said. Crying is God's way of healing people when they are sad.

"I'm very glad you can cry whenever you're sad or whenever you're angry," I said. "Sometimes daddies have a harder time showing how they feel. You know, Patrick, I wish I were more like you in that way. Someday I hope I can do better."

Patrick nodded. But in truth I held out little hope. Lifelong habits are hard to break. It would take something on the order of a miracle for me to connect with the dusty core of my own emotions. In the days before Christmas, I prayed that somehow I could be restored to at least a few of my own unshed tears.

* * *

FROM THE TIME he was an infant, my son had enjoyed an unusual passion for and affinity to music. By age four, he could pound out several bars of Wagner's "Ride of the Valkyries" by ear on the piano. More recently, he has spent countless hours singing along with the soundtrack to *The Hunchback of Notre Dame*, happily conducting during the orchestral pieces. But these were hidden pleasures for him, enjoyed in the privacy of his own room, or with the small and forgiving audience of his mother, father, and older sister, Melanie.

What the youth director of our church was suggesting was something different altogether.

"I was wondering if Patrick would sing a verse of 'Away in a Manger' during the early service on Christmas Eve," Juli Ball, the youth director, asked on our telephone answering machine.

My son's first solo. My wife and I struggled to contain our own excitement and anxiety. Catherine delicately broached the possibility, gently prodding Patrick about Juli's call, reminding him how beautifully he sang, telling him how much fun it would be. Patrick himself seemed less convinced. His face crinkled into a frown.

"You know, Mom," he said, "sometimes when I have to do something important, I get kind of scared."

Grown-ups feel that way too, he was quickly assured, but the decision to sing on Christmas Eve was left to him. Should Patrick choose to postpone his singing debut, that would be fine with his parents. His deliberations took only a few minutes.

"Okay," Patrick said, "I'll do it."

For the next week, Patrick practiced his stanza several times with his mother. A formal rehearsal at the church had also gone exceedingly well, my wife reported. But I could only envision myself at age five, singing into a microphone before hundreds of people. When Christmas Eve arrived, my expectations of my son's performance were limited indeed.

My son's solo came late in the service. By then, the spirit of the evening and many beautiful performances by young voices had thawed my inner reaches, like a Minnesota snowbank on a sunny day in March. Then Patrick and his choir took the stage. Catherine, our daughter Melanie, and I sat with the congregation in darkness as a spotlight found my son, standing alone at the microphone. He was dressed in white and wore a pair of angel wings, and he sang that night as if he had done so forever.

Patrick hit every note, slowly, confidently, and for those few moments, as his five-year-old voice washed over the people, he seemed transformed, a true angel, bestower of Christmas miracles. There was eternity in Patrick's voice that night, a penetrating beauty rich enough to dissolve centuries of manly reserve. At the sound of my son, tears welled at the corners of my eyes and spilled down my cheeks.

His song was soon over and the congregation applauded. Catherine brushed away tears. Melanie sobbed next to me. Others wept too. After the service I moved to quickly congratulate Patrick but found he had more urgent priorities.

"Mom," he said as his costume was stripped away, "I really have to go to the bathroom."

So Patrick disappeared. As he did, my friend and pastor, Dick Lord, wished me a merry Christmas. But emotion choked off my reply as the two of us embraced. Outside the sanctuary in our crowded gathering place, I received congratulations from fellow church members. But I had no time to bask there in Patrick's reflected glory. I knew I only had a short window in which to act, only a few minutes before my natural stoicism closed around my heart. I found my son as he emerged from the church bathroom.

"Patrick, I need to talk to you about something," I said, sniffling.

Alarm crossed his face.

"Is it something bad?" he asked.

"No, it's not something bad," I answered.

"Is it something good?"

"It's something very good."

I took him by the hand and led him down a long hallway, into a darkened room where we could be alone. I knelt to his height and admired his young face in the shadows, the large blue eyes, the dusting of freckles on his nose and cheeks, the dimple on one side.

He looked at my moist eyes quizzically, with concern.

"Patrick, do you remember when you asked me why you had never seen me cry?" I began. He nodded.

"Well, I'm crying now, aren't I?" I said. He nodded again.

"Why are you crying, Dad?"

"Your singing was so pretty it made me cry."

Patrick smiled proudly and flew into my arms. I began to sob.

"Sometimes," my son said into my shoulder, "life is just so beautiful you have to cry."

Our moment together was over too soon, for it was Christmas Eve, and untold treasures awaited our five-year-old beneath the tree at home. But I wasn't ready for the traditional plunge into Christmas giving just yet. I handed my wife the keys to the van and set off alone for the mile-long hike from church to our house.

The night was cool and crisp. I crossed the small park and admired the full moon hanging low over a neighborhood brightly lit in the colors of the season. As I left the park and turned up the street toward home, I met a car moving slowly down the street, a family taking in the area's Christmas lights. Someone inside rolled down a backseat window.

"Merry Christmas," a child's voice yelled out to me.

"Merry Christmas," I yelled back, and the tears began to flow once again.

—TIM MADIGAN
Arlington, Texas

Angels Among Us

T WAS SATURDAY, November 30, 1996. The day started like any other Saturday in the winter. The kids spent the morning sacked out in front of the TV, I cleaned the house, and Jim was deer hunting. For the first time, I already had the majority of my shopping finished and all the Christmas decorations were up except for the tree. So now we could sit back and enjoy the holidays.

By early afternoon, the girls and I decided to do a little shopping. We went to a nearby craft store to get supplies to make a wreath for my mom and two for ourselves. I enjoyed letting the girls help me pick out the decorations. After that we browsed in a nearby department store. By then the sky had turned dark and it was obvious a storm was coming. I've never been fond of driving in the rain, so we headed for home. Besides, I had plans to go out with some of my girl-friends and the kids were getting excited about their favorite baby-sitter, Crystal, coming over. They knew she would be ready to play Barbies and bake cookies.

The weather got much worse as we got closer to home. We were only a few miles from home when, in an instant, our lives were changed forever. It's still hard to think about, although it is one of my first thoughts in the morning and my last each night. Holly and I were only banged up a little. Heather was a different story. She took the majority of the impact from the crash. She was flown by Nightingale helicopter to the trauma center in the next town. Holly and I had to go to the local hospital first. It was awful to be torn from Heather when I wasn't sure she was going to make it to the hospital.

Jim and some family and friends met me at the local hospital and they took us to the trauma center where Heather had been taken. When we arrived, they couldn't tell us much except that they were running tests. Then the trauma specialists asked to speak to Jim and me alone. They took us to a room and closed the door. I knew it couldn't be good news and I was right. They explained to us that Heather had a closed traumatic brain injury, meaning that her brain was swollen and bleeding. She was in a coma.

Unless you have experienced something traumatic happening to your child, you can't imagine what this did to us. I've always been strong and able to suppress my emotions long enough to do what was needed to be done in emotional situations. But this time it was different. I just cried and asked, "How could this happen?"—that age-old question everyone asks when tragedy strikes.

We had a lot of questions: What does this mean? How

long will she be in a coma? Will she live? If she lives, will she be healthy? The doctors couldn't answer any of our questions. We have since learned that brain injuries are still much of a mystery to them. They can never truly predict the outcome. All they could do was watch her, keep the swelling and bleeding down, and wait for nature to take its course. All we could do was pray and then pray some more.

Suddenly our lives stopped. All the little things that seemed important before didn't mean anything now. We sat by Heather's side day and night. We left only when the nurses changed shifts and made us leave. At first we weren't to do anything to get Heather excited or agitated. All we could do was watch her. And pray. Soon she was transferred to a private room. She was still in a coma. Coma—this was still a new concept for us. Patients in a coma are not like anything you see on television. They can open their eyes, move, and even fight when they are agitated—which can be a lot of the time.

Within a week Heather had become a handful. We were encouraged to talk to her as we had always done, and to keep her stimulated. It was suggested that we talk to her about things she liked, or play music. We looked for little signs of life from her, like opening her eyes.

She started therapy and the therapist showed us different things we needed to do several times a day with Heather. All of it seemed to annoy her. Little things would disturb Heather, like more than one person talking at a time, or simply trying to brush her hair or teeth. So we had to do things quietly and gently. We continued to talk to her and play tapes she liked. Since it was Christmastime, we played Christmas music.

Around this time, Jim and I decided he should go back to work to save up his leave. The doctors still weren't sure how long Heather would be in the hospital. She was getting ready to be moved to the rehab department and could be there for a while. So he went to work each day and came to the hospital to spend the evenings and nights with us.

On December 12, 1996, Heather and I were resting in her room. I had lain down to try to take a nap since Jim and I had been up all night with her. She'd been a little restless so I had decided to play some music to calm her. I had purchased a tape by the group Alabama for her for Christmas and decided she might like to listen to it now. We had listened to the tape before and had stopped just before her favorite song, "Angels Among Us." I put the tape in and sat down to rest. Soon after the song started, I noticed tears, real tears streaming down Heather's face. I was shocked. We had always cried together when we heard this song. This was the first real sign to me that she was aware of what was happening around her. I went over to her bed and gave her a big hug and told her that everything was all right. I then said, "Mommy loves you." What happened next literally took my breath away.

In a very mumbled voice Heather said, "I love you too, Mommy." These were the most precious words I have ever heard. I was afraid my mind was playing tricks on me, so I asked her to say it again. And she said, "I love you too." I jumped on the bed and held her in my arms and we both cried. God had answered my prayers. I knew then that Heather was going to be all right. She might have to learn some things over, but she would be okay. So many people had prayed for her and their prayers were being answered.

Coming completely out of the coma was something that took days, but Heather was on her way. She didn't sleep at all that night—she talked all night. She wanted to know about her cat and her dog and even her baby sister. She could answer any questions we asked about family, friends, and things that had happened. Her memory was intact. It was slow in processing, but Heather hadn't lost her precious memories.

To see Heather today, you would never know that the accident ever happened. We have many things to thank for that. It all started with the people who stopped to help at the accident scene. They could have kept on driving but they didn't. From the very first night, the hospital was full of family and many friends who came to support, pray, and help in any and every way possible. They brought tapes, cards, stuffed animals, and Christmas decorations. A close friend, Paula, had opened an account for us at a local bank for donations to help with the medical bills and finances, since I was unable to work. People from all over sent donations, cards, letters, and gifts.

We also have the awesome power of the song "Angels Among Us" to thank. God works in many ways and I believe he worked His miracle for Heather through the power of this wonderful song. Word of this news spread fast after a local country music station heard of our wonderful Christmas miracle. What happened next was a miracle in itself.

We were already overwhelmed by the cards and gifts we had received, but when word got out of our miracle, they came in even greater abundance. Heather's room looked like a Christmas gift shop. We had hospital employees just stopping by to say "Hi" and to see the "Christmas room" they had heard so much about. Donations to our fund were unbelievable. The local radio station and two Alabama fan club members arranged for a trip for us to see and meet Alabama as soon as Heather was ready. Jim and I were again in a state of shock over this outpouring of love. People from all over the United States with their own set of problems took the time to think about ours. It restored our faith in the basic goodness of people and made us truly thankful.

Heather was discharged on December 20, 1996, less than a month after an accident that should have taken years to recover from. Today, she's on the honor roll, has started playing the clarinet in the band, is twirling baton, has joined the Girl Scouts, and is getting ready for softball season. In other words, she's back to her old self. For this we thank our family, friends (those we know and those we don't know), medical personnel, and most of all, God. They have all shown us that there truly are "angels among us."

—Penny Harcum
Suffolk, Virginia

The Kindly Veterinarian

OUR ORDEAL BEGAN early in the morning, about 6:15 A.M., December 20, 1996. My husband had just gotten out of bed when suddenly we heard our dog scratching on the hardwood floor to get our attention. Jack Dog has a history of epilepsy, and we initially thought he was having a seizure. But unlike any of his previous seizures, this time he seemed to be completely limp, unresponsive to our touch. He just lay there, motionless. His scratching on the floor seemed to have been a last-ditch plea for help.

We called a twenty-four-hour animal clinic down the street to ask advice. A staff member told us to keep an eye on him and, if he didn't get any better, to bring him in at 9:00 A.M. when the vet arrived.

Jack eventually seemed to come around; he even stood up at one point, and we thought everything would be okay. But it wasn't. He continued to act strange, wandering listlessly around the yard. When he began to pass blood, we knew we couldn't wait until nine o'clock for the vet, so I opened the phone book and found another clinic that opened at eight. I called immediately, and they told us to bring the dog right in.

My husband loaded Jack into the car and we drove him to the vet. The vet told us that he wanted to do blood tests and possibly X rays to diagnose the problem. He estimated his care would cost around four hundred dollars. After returning home and arranging to borrow some money, we called back to let the vet know he should proceed with the tests.

I went to the veterinarian's office with my mom about 10:00 A.M. Jack's prognosis was grim. At that point, our poor dog was vomiting and was in shock. The vet had determined that Jack had acute pancreatitis, possibly caused by rat poison or by something else he had ingested. We didn't keep anything like that around the house, so it was a mystery what had caused the ailment. Jack was bleeding internally, his pancreas and liver had shut down, and the vet didn't give him much chance to live. He said our only option at that point was to treat him very aggressively with intravenous fluids, blood transfusions, and antibiotics. The treatment could cost fifteen hundred dollars or more, with no guarantee that Jack would live. We knew our only option was to have him put to sleep, since it would be impossible to pay for the treatment. It was the hardest decision we ever had to make. I had my husband bring our three boys over to see Jack for the last time. We each had the chance to

THE MAGIC OF CHRISTMAS MIRACLES

give our final hugs and sad good-byes to our beloved dog. After the boys and I left, my husband stayed in the treatment room to talk with the vet.

But this kind veterinarian did not want to put Jack to sleep. He felt that he was a very special dog, so he talked my husband into giving Jack to him. He said if we signed over our ownership rights, he would do everything he could to save the dog's life. However, this meant that we could have no further contact with Jack. During treatment we would not be allowed to see him, and should he survive, he would be the property of the veterinarian. Jack meant so much to us that just the thought of him chasing a ball again, even if we weren't throwing it, was worth signing him over to the vet, so my husband got me to come back, and we agreed. We paid the bill for the office visit and the blood tests and walked out of there that day thinking we would never see our beloved Jack again.

The following Monday we called to find out if Jack had made it through the weekend. He was still very sick, but he was alive. I took his favorite ball to the vet's office and asked that they give it to him. We thought it might give Jack the incentive to keep fighting.

Without our wonderful dog, it seemed that Christmas would be anything but merry around our house. We tried to be cheerful for the kids' sake, but on Christmas Eve as we were listening to the radio play holiday music, I couldn't keep the tears away. "I'll Be Home for Christmas" was playing, and all I could think of was Jack. At about one in the afternoon, I was wrapping gifts when there was a knock at the door. My husband answered, and there was Jack, with

* 2 0 *

ribbons around his neck, and the good veterinarian wishing us a merry Christmas! The reappearance of Jack, looking happy and healthy, was truly a Christmas miracle.

We learned that the veterinarian had used his own dogs for blood transfusions, had spent the whole weekend working with Jack, and through his loving, tender care had nursed Jack back to health. This kind man had not only saved the dog, but he had also given him rabies shots, brought us a bag of special food and antibiotics, and, for all this, charged us nothing at all. He said he had just wanted to make someone's Christmas happier that year. For our family, no greater gift has ever been given. I will never forget Dr. Brian McKee of Aspen Arbor Animal Hospital in Westminster, Colorado. I never dreamed that my tears during that Christmas song would turn out to be tears of joy and gratitude for the man who brought our best friend home on Christmas Eve.

—DIAN BRADSHAW
Westminster, Colorado

And a Little Child
Shall Lead Them

 HEN YOU ARE an elementary school teacher, your classroom becomes your world. This year, a delightful young man and his classmates walked into my world and taught me some very valuable lessons about faith, miracles, and life.

Brian is part of a dynamic group of twenty-three very energetic and very bright second-graders. He is eager to learn, has a wonderful sense of humor, and has an uncanny way of seeing what's the bottom line and what's important. He also has an inoperable brain tumor and is blind, although you would never realize his limitations as he joyfully progresses through each day. Brian adores sports and keeps up with what's happening so he can "talk with the big guys" about baseball, basketball, and football. He is a caring friend to all and in return, everyone wants him as a partner and a friend.

Recently, I asked the children to write in their journals one wish that they would like to make. I told them to choose one that would be just for them. Brian wrote, in Braille, that he "would like to meet Cal Ripken [of the Baltimore Orioles] because he is a great baseball player. He is also a nice man who loves children. I want to shake his hand."

When we shared our journal entries out loud, the students in my class decided then and there that they should write to Mr. Ripken to persuade him to meet Brian. They reasoned that if he only met Brian once, he would see how special Brian is and how lucky we are to have him in our class. I told them I wasn't sure if Mr. Ripken would respond, as he was very busy, but that we would try. We worked all morning, writing, editing, and revising so that each letter said exactly what its author wanted to express. Their very persuasive letters included supporting details such as "Brian is a friend to everyone," "He cheers us up when we are down," "He used to play baseball when he had his sight but he is good at soccer and basketball too," and finally, "He can sing 'I Feel Good' like James Brown—you really ought to hear him."

After the letters were written and lovingly packed in a mailing envelope, Brian hugged me tight and said, "Mrs. Myers, I know this wish is going to come true!" At that moment, I felt uneasy and, lacking great faith, I returned his hug and said, "I sure hope so."

I couldn't sleep for the next several nights as I thought about the children's eagerness to make a wish come true for their friend and about Brian's wonderful childlike faith. Other adults had already told me, "You'll never hear— maybe you'll get a form letter or something," or "You know how busy those professional athletes are."

I began to doubt my decision as the days passed and no reply came. Each morning the children would ask, "Did we hear from Mr. Ripken?" and each day I shook my head but tried to remain hopeful with their childlike belief that a hero never lets you down. "It takes time, you know," I said. "He's very busy."

The following Sunday, I sat in church, still thinking about what I had allowed to happen. When the minister asked for prayer concerns, a series of people asked for prayers for sick relatives, for someone suffering grief, and for a baby recently born premature. All of a sudden (and I still don't know why, because I am not a public speaker) I raised my hand and stood. "I don't know if we should pray about this concern, but I don't know where else to turn," I said in a voice not my own. I proceeded to tell about Brian, his wish, and the love and concern of his classmates. The church was completely silent as I told of my dilemma. After a brief pause, the minister said that she "thought we could offer prayers for the children and Brian." I sat down as we as a church family offered this "problem" to a higher power. After church, everyone wanted to learn more about this special young man and everyone was kind but a bit skeptical, like me.

The week began with little change and with the daily barrage of questions: "Did we hear?" Then Thursday came— and our school secretary excitedly shared a call she had received from a Mr. Cal Ripken's office: we were to bring Brian at 8:45 A.M. the next day for a private meeting with Cal Ripken. It so happened that a man in my church who heard my plea the previous Sunday played basketball with Cal Ripken's agent. Touched by Brian's story, he had been able to work out a meeting for him. Six days before Christmas found us sitting in Mr. Ripken's conference room. As we waited, Brian said he thought he might ask Cal what he did in the off season. We nervously joked while Mr. Ripken's assistant went to see "if the big guy is here." Within minutes Cal Ripken, Jr., stood towering over Brian and gave him a warm, hearty handshake and welcome. He sat down on the floor next to Brian and allowed Brian to "see" how tall he was and what his hair and face "looked like." We talked about Christmas plans, families, sports, and growing up. Cal did not rush us at all and presented Brian with an autographed hat and T-shirt. Brian's brothers and my daughter were recipients of these treasures too! Mr. Ripken watched with great enjoyment while Brian sang and danced to "I Feel Good." He even wrote on the baseball he autographed, "To Brian, Teach me how to do that James Brown thing—Cal Ripken, Jr." Not to forget our class, I had brought along copies of their letters to show Cal how much Brian meant to them. Cal was deeply touched. He gave us a copy of his children's book *Count Me In* and autographed it with a personal message to our class. Cal spun Brian around on his lap in his conference chair and they both laughed aloud.

After many photographs and about one hour, it was time to go. Brian hugged Mr. Ripken and he returned the hug, saying, "Hug me as tight as you can; that's what I tell my kids." And for a long moment, a little boy and his hero embraced in a heartfelt hug.

I tell this story because so much negative is written about sports heroes and schools today. Here is a prime example of what's right about both. Mr. Ripken had nothing to gain from meeting Brian, yet he gave freely of his precious time to a special young man whose time on earth is also precious. As Brian's teacher, I want others to know that a few super-heroes do exist and that they can be positive role models in *all* aspects of their lives.

My heartfelt gratitude goes out to twenty-two caring young people who taught me that childlike faith can make miracles happen, even when big people are skeptical, and to one wonderful young man who teaches me daily that you don't need eyes to see what is really important in life.

—DEBRA TAYLOR MYERS
Randallstown, Maryland

The Tamale Tradition

 HE DAY BEFORE Christmas was a turbulent one for my sister, Carmen, a dedicated school nurse. Although the students were on vacation, their parents were not. En masse, angry and concerned parents came to the school to meet with school and county health officials to demand the expulsion of a young student alleged to have a communicable disease.

Some one hundred parents filled the lunchroom. Sitting, standing, and in huddles, their loud voices echoed threats of withdrawing their own children from school if the situation was unresolved. Their short tempers both heated and chilled the air, making me frightened for my sister. I instantly understood why I was there instead of out doing last-minute Christmas shopping. My sister needed me.

The room was devoid of holiday cheer. In fact, the only cheer was an ugly chant the parents made up: "New Year's

Day—out goes Kaye!" The debate dragged on into late afternoon.

Unable to convince the crowd that the hapless third-grader Kaye was not contagious if certain precautions were followed, and weary from the discussion, the chairperson called for a fifteen-minute break. I jumped from my front row seat to be at my sister's side should angry parents approach her during the break. Sure enough, several did. Quickly I ushered my sister into the kitchen cove and locked the door behind us.

"A little like when we were kids, only reversed," I said, twinkling at my oldest, most educated sister. Reared in the barrio, we shared plenty of childhood memories of having to stick together for sisterly survival. We laughed together, relishing the temporary relief from the stress of the day.

My sister glanced down at her watch. "A quarter to six! How did it get to be so late! And the market closes at six! Here," she said, shoving a wad of bills into my hand, "go pick up the tamale *masa* (dough) for me. Tonight is tamale night."

"But I can't leave you here alone!" I argued.

"There's no time to argue, little sister," she said, assuming the big sister role. "Tonight is tamale night, and you know it's not Christmas without tamales. Now go!"

I left reluctantly. Reluctant to leave her alone with a hostile crowd of parents, but just as reluctant to try to find the market she was sending me to. My sister lives in one part of town, I live in another. Where did she say this store was? Did she say Jessie's Market? Or Jesus's Market? I decided it had to be Jesus (pronounced *hey-sus* in Spanish), only because Jesus is a special and well-loved name in our culture. So out I went into the cold Christmas night, in an unfamiliar and not exactly nice part of town, concerned for both my sister's safety and my own. With the words "It's not Christmas without tamales" as my rallying cry, I went out into the night in search of the dough.

Oh, how well I knew the Christmas tamale tradition. As the oldest sister of seven siblings, Carmen was obligated to host the annual event. Thankfully, I was the youngest and would never have to be in charge! By my calculations, Carmen had been doing this for twenty-five Christmases in a row. Why did she persist after all these years? Well, those who have tasted authentic tamales can testify to the pleasure of the experience. And my sister the matriarch, like all matriarchs, was hopelessly hooked on tradition.

In a labor of love, the upholder of the tamale tradition spends hours shopping for the right ingredients and hours more measuring, stirring, and cooking the ultimate Christmas tamales. And every year the families—through some finely honed tamale instinct—arrive at just the right moment, the moment when the aroma of chile-drenched meat fills the kitchen. Decked out in Christmas gold taffetas and red and black velvets, the throng of grandparents, parents, and children wait like royalty for the first tamales to roll off the line. But more than just satisfying our stomachs, the tamale tradition saturates our souls with the love of reunion with family. Warm, big bear hugs. Young and old eyes opened wide to gaze at the carefully wrapped presents under the tree. The little ones flocking to the Nativity scene, to take turns holding the little baby Jesus. Everyone is refreshed by the renewal of the family connection and leaves tamale night with a renewed sense of belonging, a sense so vital today to our busy individual lives.

So there I was, driving unfamiliar streets in order not to break that connection. Driving around the block for the third time, I finally spotted the corner and alley that my sister described. This must be it, I thought as I parked my car on the side of the street and ran for the door of the store. As I reached for the door handle I looked up, and only then did I notice the big orange CLOSED sign swinging in the window. It was after six o'clock.

I banged on the door. I had to get that tamale dough! It's not Christmas without tamales! Through the glass door I could see quite plainly into the store. Two teenage girls stood together behind the counter, counting money at an old-fashioned register. They scowled at me, shaking their heads and mouthing the words "We're closed" before avoiding my gaze again. What was wrong with these young girls? Didn't they know about the tamale tradition? Didn't they care? So eager to go out for the night with their boyfriends, they could not be bothered by a tradition-bound woman pounding on their door in search of tamale dough. Who needs tradition on a special night like Christmas Eve? One girl crossed the room and pulled the shade down over the window. Good-bye, old woman.

I slumped to the icy sidewalk in front of the door. I had failed. The tamale tradition would end with me. Suddenly, I heard footsteps. They seemed to come from nowhere on the darkened street. Trouble! I struggled to my feet, ready to run back to my car. Two arm lengths away stood a tall, thin man with a beard. Help me God, I prayed silently. The man watched me silently. Finally he asked me in Spanish, "*¿Que pasa, mija?*" (What's happening, my child?)

I burst into tears as I poured out the evening's misfortunes, blowing my nose at the end of every sentence and ending with ". . . and it's not Christmas without tamales!"

Without a word, the thin man reached into his jacket pocket and pulled out a set of keys. He unlocked the door and held it open for me to enter. "Don't worry my child, I will help you. You will have your tamales after all. It is me—Jesus."

—BETTINA FLORES
Granite Bay, California

Smokey and the Minister

 Y SISTER AND I wanted only one thing for
Christmas the year of 1987: a kitten. My par-
ents had asked at veterinary clinics and looked in the paper,
but there wasn't a kitten to be had in Gunnison, Colorado.
By chance, they learned that friends of theirs who lived in
Lake City, a town fifty-five miles southwest of Gunnison,
recently had found a three-month-old kitten wandering by
their lake. I remember our delight when on Christmas Eve,
a little gray fur ball with big yellow eyes arrived. Smokey
immediately became a treasured member of the family.

Smokey was a patient, loving animal from the beginning.
My sister and I loved to dress him in doll clothes and push
him around in the baby stroller. He tolerated this with amazing patience and each night slept curled at my mom's feet.
Independent by nature, Smokey loved to be outside. He
would roam the neighborhood and the open fields in front
of our house. When we moved to Longmont, Colorado, in

1991 this habit did not change. Smokey went exploring every day, but he always came in to cuddle at night.

Seven years after we got him, near Thanksgiving of 1994, for the first time in his life, Smokey did not come home. We called and called all evening, but no Smokey. The next morning, hearing a yellow moving truck start its motor, my mother, on impulse, ran across the street and asked the driver if she'd seen our gray cat. No, she hadn't, and with a wave, she drove away. We didn't see Smokey at all the rest of the day or the next, and we began to worry. We posted signs around the neighborhood and called the local Humane Society. No luck. One afternoon, I walked all around the area calling for my cat and was so disappointed, I cried myself to sleep.

Two weeks after Smokey disappeared, our neighbor walked across the street and told us quietly that our cat was in Florida. Apparently, he had climbed aboard the moving van while it was parked across the street. Trapped in the dark for seven days without food or water, Smokey had enough energy left to bolt out of the truck as soon as the doors were opened. Our neighbor's friends saw only a streak of gray disappear into the Bradenton neighborhood.

When we heard the news that our cat was two thousand miles away, we were devastated. Although it was good to know he was still alive, we also realized we probably wouldn't ever see him again. We tried to adjust to the fact that our cat was gone. Occasionally, though, our neighbor would walk across the street to tell us that her friends had seen our cat in their Florida neighborhood again. This gave us hope. My mother called a few animal shelters in Bradenton to see if anyone had recently picked up a gray cat. After she had tried for ten minutes to explain the situation to one man on the other end of the line, he said, "Now your cat is where?"

"My cat's in Bradenton," my mom said helplessly.

"And where are you?"

"I'm in Colorado."

When at last he understood, he asked, "Does he have any distinguishing marks?"

"No, he's just gray all over."

"Well, ma'am," he said in an apologetic voice, "I've got about one hundred cats in here and probably twenty of them are gray."

"But his name is Smokey," my mom said desperately.

"Well, ma'am, that tends to work better with dogs than with cats."

There seemed to be nothing more we could do, but our neighbor's friends kept seeing him. Coupled with the repeated sightings was the knowledge that Smokey was a one-family cat. He loved us very much, but he didn't take well to strangers. We knew he wouldn't go looking to the people of Bradenton for help. If we didn't find him, he would be on his own. Resolutely, we began pricing plane tickets. It was an improbable chance, but we had to try. Five days before Christmas and six weeks after Smokey had disappeared, we found an inexpensive fare and my dad boarded a plane for Florida.

My father is an Episcopal priest, and he had only two days to look for Smokey before he had to return for Christmas

Eve services. He arrived in Florida, rented a car, and checked into a motel room. The next day, he drove to the neighborhood where Smokey had been sighted and spent the morning calling for our cat. He wore his clerical collar so no one would think he was out casing houses. At noon, he ate a quick lunch and called a few shelters, one of which had picked up a gray cat. He went to look but it wasn't Smokey. That afternoon, he was back walking the streets, calling, "Smokey! Kitty, kitty, kitty!" An old man mowing his lawn asked my dad what he was doing and offered to lend him his bicycle to help him look. Dad thanked him but declined, thinking he'd have better luck on foot. A woman working outside told my dad that her husband had seen a gray stray earlier that day. With renewed hope, he walked on and kept calling: "Smokey! Kitty, kitty, kitty!" Suddenly there was a rustling in the bushes to the left. He called again: "Smokey?" A gray shape appeared with a tentative "meow?" And there he was.

My father picked up a thin, ragged, but affectionate Smokey and held him. He was afraid that Smokey might be skittish or might not recognize him, but that was not the case. Smokey knew my father immediately and had no intention of moving once he was safely in his arms. Even back at the motel, he was constantly either rubbing up against my father's legs or sitting in his lap.

There was no shortage of tears when my father called home with the news. "Girls!" my mom called excitedly, "Daddy found him!" The three of us crowded around the receiver, and over the phone came a familiar "meow."

But all was not smooth sailing yet. When Smokey and my father arrived at the airport, a problem arose. The airline wouldn't allow Smokey on the plane without proof of his latest vaccination. My dad immediately called home and my mother called our vet. Fortunately, he was in the office and able to fax the information to my father in time for him to make his flight. Smokey, though on the plane, had to ride in the baggage compartment. My father had to change planes in New Orleans and Houston, and he could only hope Smokey was making the connections as well. It was a relief when he found Smokey waiting in the baggage claim at Denver.

It was after midnight when Smokey finally arrived home. My sister and I were asleep and didn't see our traveling cat until morning. My mother related the story of his homecoming: My father brought the cat carrier upstairs, set it on the bed, and opened it. Smokey walked out, looked around, jumped off the bed, and ran downstairs. A little later, as my dad shared the details of his trip, Smokey jumped back up on the bed, circled it a few times, and curled up beside my mom, just as if he'd never been away.

After surgery for an infected wound, and the indignity of wearing a big plastic collar for a few weeks to keep him from scratching his wound, Smokey was back to his normal weight. Previously so independent, he now became more affectionate. Even three and a half years later, if any of us sits down for any length of time, Smokey is on our lap. He currently sleeps at my feet at night.

No one can tell me that miracles don't happen. Smokey

is sitting beside me at this very minute because of several. I will always remember the joy of seeing my cat again. For the second time in his life, Smokey had come home for Christmas.

—EMILY HOULIK
Longmont, Colorado

Snow Angels

FEW DAYS BEFORE last Christmas, I ran over a boy on a sled. He flew out of nowhere during the season's first serious snowstorm, a small figure darting down a steep farmyard into the road just as my Blazer came over a knoll. Through the veil of snow, I caught only the briefest glimpse of him before I sharply cut the wheel—a pale oval, an impression of startled eyes behind eyeglasses, a blue parka.

I remember hearing the awful crunch, a muffled cry, and then my truck was sliding down a steep incline, plowing sideways through deep drifts, coming to rest almost on its side. I became aware of a hissing sound, thought it was a broken radiator, then saw the source: a shattered bottle of Diet Pepsi lying on the passenger-side window. The groceries I had just purchased were all over the place. I remember staring at a burst box of berry-flavored Kix on the dashboard and thinking, absurdly, how awfully disappointed my five-year-old daughter was going to be.

How long did I sit there? Perhaps no more than ten seconds. It felt like ten minutes. Then I ripped off my shoulder belt, kicked open the door with my boot, climbed out, and clawed my way through the knee-deep snow back up the bank. The boy was lying in the middle of the road, eerily still, crying softly, "My legs. My legs. I can't move my legs." The snow was pouring down like cinders from heaven.

As I crouched at his side, I remember thinking two things with almost military clarity. Number one, I had to get him out of the road or we would both be run over by the next vehicle that came over the knoll. Number two, this kid was possibly going to die or at least never walk again because I had driven over his legs, crushed his back, God knows what.

As I knelt there, a flood of soft paternal words began flowing from my mouth: "Listen to me, son. Listen. You're going to be okay. But you have to lie still and let me get help. First we have to get you to the side of the road. Can you hear me? You will be okay. Trust me. Try and relax. Breathe deep. Everything will be fine." I don't know whom I was trying to convince most.

He closed his eyes, nodded, and I placed my arms under his limp body and moved him gently to the shoulder, aware that I could be doing even more damage—severing what was left of a shattered spinal cord or destroying whatever muscle tissue or nerve connections remained. But the snow was coming down so hard and visibility was so poor that I imagined a plow truck roaring over the knoll at any second, bearing down on us both like some rampaging prehistoric beast.

"Can you move your fingers?" I said.

"Yes," he replied and showed me. Snowflakes were accumulating and melting on his flushed face. I studied his eyes to see if he was slipping into shock. His eyes were clear. He was a good-looking kid, I realized, maybe twelve or thirteen. Damn brave.

Then from behind us rose a heartrending wail. I turned and saw a large coatless woman struggling through the snow, crying, "Oh my God, oh my God!" Two children were in her wake. She lost her footing and tumbled into the drift at the bottom of the driveway. I went to help her out, extending her my hand and pulling her from the drift. Her face was a mask of anguish, the face of a mother confronted with the unthinkable. We stood there in each other's odd embrace for a moment, performing a little minuet on the slippery road, staring briefly into each other's eyes until we heard a small sound and simultaneously turned to the boy.

He was standing up.

"It's okay, Mom," he said, rubbing his back. "I think I'm okay."

His name was Matthew, like the tax collector-turned-apostle. He was the son of a church caretaker. He sat on a chair in his mother's warm kitchen holding back sobs. "Why are you crying, Matthew?" asked his mother. "Are you injured?"

"No," he said with a trembling voice. "I was just thinking I could have been killed. I don't know why I wasn't killed."

His younger sister Sarah explained what happened. When

school was called off for the day, they'd gone into the back meadow to ride sleds. The farm's steeper front yard had eventually tempted them. They never even considered the danger of the road. I consoled him. We're all entitled to a few stupid stunts. Hopefully we survive them.

"But I could have been killed," Matthew repeated in a kind of daze. "I don't know why I wasn't killed."

"Because we were both incredibly lucky," I answered.

"I think it was a miracle," said his mother.

I went outside to watch the wrecker truck winch my truck out of the ditch. Both tires flattened, a bent fender. A small price to pay for an astonishing piece of luck. "Frankly," said the town constable, indicating the intersecting skid pattern and sled track, "I don't see how you missed running clean over him, it's amazing."

"Damn near a miracle, I'd say," piped up the driver of the wrecker.

I went back to say good-bye to Matthew and his mother. He'd gone to lie down, and his mother thanked me profusely. We actually embraced, and she began to cry. I told her I would call in a day or so to see how everyone was doing.

"Are you okay?" she asked, studying me.

"Yes, I'm fine," I replied.

But I wasn't. In fact, I was more deeply shaken than I have ever been in my life. I knew that the boy had disappeared directly under the front of my truck yet somehow had survived with only an angry red welt on the small of his back to show for it. I couldn't explain it. I might have said it was a miracle, if I believed in such things. But miracles in our time have always struck me as the cheap parlor tricks of faith—something done by Vegas-style preachers to keep the crowd interested and the tithes flowing.

I went home and sat for a couple of hours in our den watching chickadees dive-bomb our bird feeder. I didn't feel like moving, didn't feel like talking. My wife took our two young children out Christmas shopping. As I watched the birds feed, the movie projector between my ears played the accident over and over.

The snow stopped. It got dark. The children came home, bathed, and went to bed. I went up and kissed them and came down and turned on the evening news. Twenty children had died from a Serb mortar shell in a playground during a holiday truce in Sarajevo. A mall in New Jersey had obtained a court injunction to keep the Salvation Army Santas from offending potential customers. Two more foreign tourists had been gunned down in Florida.

I turned the channel and discovered Jimmy Stewart arguing with a cherub-cheeked gent named Clarence, who claimed to be his guardian angel. I've seen It's a Wonderful Life maybe thirty times, and it's never failed to put a lump in my throat. It's about a man who doesn't believe in miracles until he experiences one.

Before I hit the boy on the sled, I had been having what my wife calls my "annual Christmas crisis," a private little tempest of the soul that begins somewhere around the winter solstice, when darkness descends like a closing curtain and news programs flood the tube with specials on the year's most memorable events, usually the most sensational human and natural disasters.

It was worse than ever, I think, because I am a journalist who has written more than my share of stories illustrating man's contempt for his neighbor and his planet. I was weary of being a trafficker in the misfortune of others, although it had taken a recent "golden opportunity" for me to realize this. An editor called me and asked if I would write a book about serial killers. The advance was eye-opening. He was surprised when I passed on the offer. To tell the truth, I was surprised too. As career moves go, this was tantamount to leaving Congress to join a jug band.

Call me stupid—definitely poorer—but if I couldn't stop the tragedies of the world, I reasoned, at least I wouldn't contribute to the roar of white noise coming down the information highway. I would write about happier things—golf, for example, and gardening.

But in spite of my decision, on the morning of the big snowstorm I was still in a funk. I wondered why. The autumn had been glorious, my rose beds were lush; I'd even agreed to play carols on my guitar at the Christmas Eve service.

The answer came to me slowly. You can take the journalist out of the world, but you can't take the world out of the journalist. As the days shortened, the old year's grisly toll poured forth from the newsstands and blackened my new determination to enjoy the season of light.

And so, at the height of the storm both without and within, disgusted with my disgust, I decided to go to the grocery store. It was empty save for a lone clerk totaling the items of an elderly woman in the checkout line. She was buying a copy of *People* and a potted poinsettia. I noticed she was wearing running shoes instead of boots. She smiled at me and said, "It's beautiful outside, isn't it? But you know, some people always drive too fast when it's snowing." I smiled and agreed. Kooky old bird. I got back into my Blazer and headed for home. Turning onto Meadow Cross Road, however, I kept thinking about what she had said. As I approached the knoll by the farm, I cut my speed by half and turned my head to admire the lovely snowfall blanketing the world. I looked back just as the boy on the sled flew under my wheels.

How do you say thank you to someone who enters your life for fifteen seconds? All I know about her is that she likes celebrities and flowers and could use some new boots for Christmas.

On Christmas Eve morning I walked down the hill to fetch the mail and almost keeled over. The same issue of *Time* that contained its IMAGES OF '93—a slick collage of war, famine, fire, and urban violence—had on its cover a painting of an angel from the National Museum of American Art. THE NEW AGE OF ANGELS, read the cover headline. WHAT IN HEAVEN IS GOING ON?

I skipped straight over the pictorial mayhem to page 56 and started reading: "In her best-selling collection of angel encounters, *A Book of Angels*, author Sophy Burnham writes that angels disguise themselves, as a dream, a comforting presence, a pulse of energy, a person—to ensure that the message is received, even if the messenger is explained away. 'It is not that skeptics do not experience the mysterious and divine,' she explains, 'but rather that the mysteries are presented to them in such a flat and factual, everyday, reasonable way so as not to disturb.'"

Once again, I sat in my den watching chickadees, mulling this over. I considered the possibility that my guardian angel—my Clarence—was an old lady in Nikes who thought the world would be a better place if we all slowed down and noticed the passing scenery. But then it was time to go to church.

The service was held in a freezing barn, with real sheep and a bracing air of fresh manure—just the kind of place you'd expect the Son of Man to pick for a nursery suite. An overflow crowd, mostly families with children, heard Saint Matthew's account of the virgin birth, and I played my guitar. As we went back out into the night, the snow began to fall, as if on cue, yet I couldn't help thinking that a peaceful scene in New England is a tableau of terror in Bosnia.

At home Maggie suddenly let go of my hand and ran and flopped down in the yard. Her younger brother, Jack, followed on her heels, falling with his arms joyously outspread. "Look, Daddy," Maggie cried out, "snow angels!"

Frankly, I'd completely forgotten about snow angels. But I think the snow angels my children made last Christmas Eve were outstanding. Even more amazing, in the morning, they were still there.

—JAMES DODSON
Topsham, Maine

The Other Christmas Box

HEN I WAS growing up, birthdays were the best day of the year. I became Queen for a Day and could choose my favorite breakfast in the morning and dinner at night. There was always a pile of presents, but that wasn't as important as being treated like the most important person in the world. Christmas was fun, but birthdays were even better! It was the day that belonged to me alone.

Somewhere in the shuffle of growing up, I had failed to comprehend the real meaning of Christmas. Perhaps I had been taught what the day represented somewhere along the line, but to me, Christmas was simply Santa and stockings and presents. If there were a baby and a manger anywhere in all our traditions, my young mind had gotten the reindeer mixed in with the sheep and cattle in the stable, and the story of the first Christmas held little significance in my life.

When I was about six years old, I remember suddenly

becoming aware that Christmas was actually the day Jesus was born—it was His birthday. I'm not sure how it was brought to my attention, but I was amazed! I had never before understood that it was His birth we celebrated each year. But now that it was clear, there was one thing that troubled me: If it was really Jesus's birthday, why didn't anyone give Him presents? Why didn't He get the royal treatment I received on my birthdays? So, unbeknown to anyone, including my parents, I made up my mind to get something to give to Jesus on his birthday. It seemed the only proper thing to do, and I became obsessed with making sure He had as wonderful a birthday as I enjoyed every year. The question was, what should I give Him?

I lived in a town with only a few stores, the nearest and biggest being a Woolworth. With every penny and nickel I had been able to save for weeks clutched tightly in my hand, I made my trek down the dirt road to Woolworth. I scanned every aisle, every shelf—brushes, handkerchiefs, pens, tools, towels, Christmas lights, candy canes—but there was nothing that seemed just right. I came home disappointed but still determined to find the perfect gift for Him.

After days of agonizing worry, it was Christmas Eve and I still had no gift for Jesus. As I searched my own bedroom, I suddenly found the answer. It was a little silver bracelet of mine with ten shiny round charms hanging from it. On each charm was engraved one of the Ten Commandments. I knew there was some connection between Jesus and the Ten Commandments and felt certain He would love it! I carefully put it in a little box, wrapped it by myself, and put a card on top which read, "Happy Birthday to Jesus, from Hope. I love you." I remember feeling that this was my own little secret. I was afraid someone might laugh at my idea, so I decided to hide it in the top drawer of my dresser. I couldn't even see in the drawer, but on tiptoes, I reached as high as I could and pushed the box to the farthest corner of the drawer, safely hidden under my T-shirts. In my believing heart, I was certain Jesus would find it there Christmas morning.

The next morning, I dashed into the living room with my sisters and brother to a tree buried in presents and stockings filled to the brim. Christmas was as enchanting as ever, and it took us an hour or more to unwrap every present. But even in all the excitement of new toys and games, I couldn't stop thinking about the box hidden in my bedroom. I could hardly wait until the last present was opened, and then I quietly walked into my bedroom to make sure Jesus had found his birthday gift.

Once again, on tiptoe, I stretched and pushed my anxious fingers under the pile of clean clothes. There, in the quiet of my bedroom, I felt the box. The moment my fingers touched it, a feeling of warmth and wonder filled my body. It was an unmistakable sweetness confirming the fact that Jesus had not only found the box, but that He loved it. At the same moment, I also understood that He had left it there for a purpose—He wanted me to keep it so I would remember Him and think of Him every day. My whole body was tingling as this message of peace was given to me—there wasn't an ounce of disappointment that He hadn't taken the box because the message was so clear to me. The emotions I felt that day at age six are still hard to describe, but I knew as much as I knew anything else that I had made Jesus very happy.

This story has been quietly tucked in my heart for over forty years, but the tangible feeling of that morning is still with me every time I remember touching that little Christmas box. My Christmases are busy and full now. There are always too many presents underneath our tree for our six children, but I have tried, in a small way, to provide my family with an experience that might capture those same tender feelings for them.

Every year for the past twenty-five years, on the first Sunday in December, I have gathered my children together and we try to think of presents we can give Jesus for his birthday. We write them down, wrap them up, and place them on the branches of our Christmas tree. We don't give bracelets or material things because we figure it all belongs to Him anyway. Instead we give gifts of the heart—the gift of trying to be a little more patient with a brother or sister or the gift of helping a recently widowed neighbor. And every Christmas as we share those gifts with one another, I have the distinct impression that Jesus accepts those gifts from us, and He smiles. I know He's having a good birthday because of all those around the world who love Him, and in their individual ways, remember Him.

—HOPE GARDNER
Mesa, Arizona

The Piano

NE COLD DECEMBER morning a few years back, my husband, Mark, and I were driving to the airport. We were headed to the West Coast to speak at a medical convention. As we voiced our anticipation of warm weather and the excitement of the big city, Mark dashed into a convenience store to purchase some last-minute items. He returned with a small brown package in his hand and a shivering elderly lady at his side.

What a contrast the two of them were—Mark in a gray wool pinstriped suit, and the stranger clothed in a green polyester coat with two missing buttons and a tan stain on the front. Her ten half-frozen toes peeked out from timeworn sandals.

As the determined woman struggled into the backseat of the car, she flashed a tender smile. "My name's Kathleen," she announced boldly. "I understand you folks are headed down Kentucky way."

Her husband, it turned out, was a patient at a nearby nursing home, and was not expected to survive through the Christmas holidays. The two had married late in life, never had any children, and when their small monthly allotment dwindled, Kathleen often hitched a ride to the nursing home. Like so many Appalachian women of her generation, Kathleen was fiercely independent, a survivor. She usually stayed at the nursing home all day, for even though her husband was in a coma, the facility was warm, the food was good, and there was a piano in the dayroom where she could while away the hours and her cares at the keyboard.

As we approached the small brick convalescence center, I remembered the cache of calling cards in my briefcase. I handed my ivory linen card to Kathleen. "Don't hesitate to call us if we can ever give you a lift to the nursing home," I said. Kathleen smiled, thanked us for the ride, then confronted the unyielding wind, her thin coat blowing wildly.

As we drove off, our thoughts shifted to the activities ahead. The program was sure to be professionally stimulating, not to mention the lure of great shopping during "down" time.

When we returned home, baking, buying gifts, and an endless array of holiday errands consumed our days. Kathleen called a couple of times to chat, but it wasn't until Christmas that our paths actually crossed again.

"Did you take Kathleen anything for Christmas?" Mark asked late Christmas night. How could I have forgotten?

We scurried about the house gathering some remnants of Christmas for Kathleen. Surprisingly, as we approached her tiny frame residence, the porch light was still burning, a beacon in the dark night. We rang the doorbell and waited. Soon, Kathleen opened the door and invited us in, saying she just knew we were coming for Christmas.

As we stepped inside the living room, we took in Kathleen's short-sleeved cotton dress, the tattered sofa and chair, and rugs taped around each window to protect her from harsh weather. A bare bulb dangled from a ceiling wire, scarcely lighting the room.

"This is Honey. She's an alley cat plus a better breed," Kathleen announced, stroking the animal's soft yellow fur. "And Honey and I have a special present for you." Kathleen picked up a xylophone and methodically plunked out "We Wish You a Merry Christmas" on its rusted, paint-chipped keys. "I found this for a quarter last summer at a rummage sale," she said proudly, "and I've been saving it for just the right occasion. Got this dress there, too. A real bargain for a dime, and a perfect fourteen at that.

"Do you have a piano?" Kathleen asked us. I nodded, feeling uncomfortable about the grand piano in our living room at home and the nice clothes in our closets. Christmas was nearly over, and in my busyness I hadn't even played a Christmas carol. In our pursuit of the things money could buy, it seemed we had overlooked many of the things it couldn't buy.

"Could you . . . would you go home and play 'Silent Night'? You could hold the telephone next to your piano and I could celebrate Christmas one more time," Kathleen pleaded. Then she shared with us her dream of finding a piano, preferably an old upright model like the one she'd played as a child. She had little money, but she had faith that God would send one her way.

After the holidays, I combed the classifieds in hopes of buying a used piano for Kathleen. It soon became apparent, though, that all the bargains had been snatched up by area piano dealers. I tried to compensate with other small gifts—a pretty blouse, an African violet, a tin of talcum powder.

On Valentine's Day, Kathleen hardly noticed the chocolates I brought her. "My piano will be here soon," she insisted. And throughout the months, Kathleen's faith intensified. Her strong faith in the midst of poverty was an unsettling paradox; it amazed, yet amused me. I feared that disappointment rather than a piano was coming her way.

But later that spring, something wonderful happened, and Mark and I dropped by to tell Kathleen what we'd learned. Some family members were moving and had sold their home. The new owner's sole request was that the heavy upright piano in the basement be promptly removed from the premises.

"Can you think of anyone who could use that old relic?" they had asked. "It's theirs, if they move it." Could we ever!

Kathleen ran to meet us when she spotted our car. "My piano . . . it's coming. . . . I had a dream last night. It's coming from a little town I've never heard of near Point Pleasant, West Virginia," she squealed.

"God's not too far off," Mark mumbled, maintaining a reserved amazement for God's handiwork. The piano was indeed located in a tiny, postage-stamp-sized town only thirty miles from Point Pleasant.

Mark and I could hardly contain our joy. Kathleen was baffled—not that a piano was coming, but that we were surprised. For she had been joyfully expectant since Christmas night, when she put her faith into action. "I've been playing my piano already in my mind," she explained. "Without faith, we can't please God, you know."

Ever since the massive oak upright was rolled into Kathleen's living room, music hasn't stopped flowing. Artistic expression hasn't been limited by her advancing age, debilitating arthritis, or glaucoma. Kathleen's husband has since passed away and Honey had to be put to sleep. But music—be it the classics, Roaring Twenties tunes, or gospel songs recalled from childhood tent meetings—connects Kathleen with the world. She accompanies the congregation at her neighborhood church and joined a senior citizens' band. Kathleen doesn't read music, but she listens to tapes, the radio, and other musicians, and beautifully emulates what she hears.

Before I met Kathleen, I understood faith in my mind; now I understand it in my heart. For as with all acts of faith, Kathleen's Christmas miracle happened not when she received, but the moment she first believed.

—VICTORIA HANSEN
Prestonsburg, Kentucky

The Gift of Love

HERE ARE MOMENTS in our lives that stand out like precious gems. Some are anticipated, planned for, and recorded. Sometimes they are given to us— singular events that change the way we view our world and our lives. In December of 1990, I was given a gift of love and hope of such magnitude that it changed the course of my life. The giver of this momentous gift was my golden retriever, Kelly.

In late 1989, I was editor of the newsletter of the Golden Retriever Club of Illinois. Our club was searching for ways to attract new members. I read several articles about dogs visiting sick and elderly people in nursing homes and hospitals. The stories about these dogs and the work they did made me think this type of program might fit in nicely with our club and would be an excellent way to involve owners of pet-quality golden retrievers.

By December of 1990, the fledgling therapy dog program

of the Golden Retriever Club of Illinois was ready to go. We had groups in place in several Chicago area suburbs. Now, just before Christmas, Kelly and I were about to make our first visit to a local residential home for mentally disabled women.

I was a nervous wreck the day of our visit. Two other club members were with me. They both had conformation-quality goldens, and one of the dogs was quite skilled at obedience work. Although these women were friends of mine, I was feeling quite inferior. Kelly was neither conformation quality nor an obedience competitor. I was becoming more certain by the minute that I had made a terrible mistake thinking Kelly could hold her own against two such remarkable goldens as my friends'.

The skies were overcast, the temperature hovered in the thirties, and the gray day seemed to match my mood perfectly as I drove the short distance to the home. None of us had done anything like this before, and all the discussions we had had in preparation for the visit suddenly seemed meaningless. We did not know what to expect from the residents, and the strange sights and sounds inside the facility added to our apprehension.

Perhaps we had made a mistake. Although our dogs had been tested and registered with Therapy Dogs International, maybe they weren't ready for this. Then we saw several of the residents hurrying down the hallway toward us, smiling. It was too late to turn back. We all took deep breaths, smiled encouragingly at each other, gripped the dogs' leads tightly in our hands, and walked into the first of seven cottages we were to visit.

Many of the women in the brightly lit, cheerfully furnished dayroom seemed very ill. Several of them were in wheelchairs, some secured so they wouldn't fall out. A few women were sitting on sofas or chairs placed in cozy groupings about the room. A brightly colored rag rug added a homey touch, and a small Christmas tree sat in one corner, awaiting decorations. As we entered the room, the dogs took over and began going from group to group, almost demanding to be petted. The women were happy to oblige.

As the dogs circulated amid the joyous laughter and excited chatter of the group, Kelly gravitated toward a woman seated in a wheelchair off to one side. As we approached her, I noticed that she appeared to be sleeping. Kelly was determined to attract her attention, and since she was in the dayroom with the other women, I assumed it would be okay for Kelly to approach her.

Kelly walked up to the wheelchair and pushed her soft golden head under the woman's arm. Nothing happened. Kelly pushed harder. Still nothing. Kelly put her muzzle up against the woman's cheek and bestowed one of her precious kisses—cold, wet, and very sloppy. That did it! The woman opened her eyes, focused very slowly on Kelly, and began to make some rather loud and alarming noises—alarming to me, at least. Kelly's tail wagged faster than I had ever seen. She continued to lick the woman on the cheek and seemed very pleased with herself.

The woman reached out to pull Kelly closer, which proved difficult because she had very limited arm movement. She did succeed in bringing Kelly's head closer to hers. The noises she was making stopped, and she began to croon, "My baby! My baby!" over and over again.

One of the nurses, who had been watching the other dogs, heard the commotion Kelly had started and hurried toward us, visibly shaken. What had we done? Had Kelly upset this woman? Maybe I shouldn't have allowed Kelly to kiss her.

"Mary Ann? Mary Ann? Can you hear me?" the nurse shouted in the woman's ear. Mary Ann's eyes flickered toward the nurse, but she never stopped her crooning and pulled even harder at Kelly's head. The nurse glanced at me. There were tears in her eyes.

"Mary Ann is in the final stages of Alzheimer's disease," the nurse explained. "She has not said one word in two and a half years. In fact, we didn't know she still could speak. She has been semiconscious and hasn't responded to anyone or anything all that time. And look at her! She's laughing and talking to your dog!"

By now, several other nurses were aware of what was happening between Kelly and Mary Ann, and they came over to marvel at the momentous event and to admire Kelly. Mary Ann continued to hug Kelly and to talk to her, repeating the same words again and again. For more than five minutes, Mary Ann and Kelly continued to interact. Then suddenly, Mary Ann's eyes closed, her arm fell at her side and she slept once more.

The nurse explained that Mary Ann's condition was progressive; nothing could be done to slow or stop it. No one had expected Mary Ann to "wake up," but she had. For slightly more than five minutes, Mary Ann had been awake, had known she was still alive and that there was someone with her who loved her. This was Kelly's gift at Christmas to a stranger named Mary Ann.

Our visit continued, and we took our dogs to other cottages and visited with the rest of the residents. The dogs put on a little show, wore silly Santa hats, and gave as much love as they received.

Throughout the afternoon, my mind kept going back to the scene with Mary Ann. I turned it over and over, reliving it, cherishing it. As I watched the other two dogs work with Kelly to bring a few moments of love and joy to these women, I thought of what I had seen and felt in those few brief moments. I realized then that I would never trade all the competition blue ribbons in the world for the time I had spent that day watching Kelly's love work its special magic for Mary Ann and the others.

How privileged I am, I thought, to have Kelly in my life. How lucky I am to have witnessed today's events. Moments in our lives are like precious gems. Sometimes they come when we least expect them—serendipitous gifts of the heart or soul, even from such a candidate as a family dog. Such a moment was given to me by Kelly. No, she is not show quality. She is a pet and starting to gray a little with age. But with her, I was able one Christmas to rediscover the special warmth and gentle love that comes from bringing joy to others.

—GLORIA S. DITTMAN
Lake Zurich, Illinois

The Postman Who
Saved Christmas

Our first collection, Christmas Miracles, *included the heart-warming story "The Town That Gave Christmas." A reader in Canada realized that her family had been telling that same story for generations, but from the viewpoint of her grandfather. He was the postman who had delivered the gifts. We are pleased to include her family's story here.*

 HRISTMAS EVE WAS a festive event at the Schow home in Cardston, Alberta, Canada. Traditions were alive and well as the eight children, ages three to sixteen, bustled around helping their mother Ingeborg with the many preparations for the season. My mother Ruth was only eight at the time but still remembers all the activity. There was the famous Schow Danish fudge and homemade toffee to be made and the stretch candy to be pulled. In the midst of the merriment the back door suddenly flung open with a bang. An icy blast of cold wind and snow invaded the cozy kitchen. Sidney, fifteen, had arrived home from his paper route. He was bone-cold and glad to be finally in the warmth of the family home. Rex helped him haul a final load of coal and wood into the house to keep the family's wonderful cast-iron stove going for the rest of the night.

Nineteen twenty-seven was one of the coldest winters this little town had seen, and the Depression had families scrambling to be frugal and resourceful. The Schow family owned a couple of cows and a few chickens, which helped to supply milk, eggs, cream, and butter to their larder. George Schow was a talented man with carpenter skills who had even made a wooden cheese press so the family could make its own cheese.

In the late afternoon, the children gathered around the piano to sing Christmas carols. They were anticipating the arrival of their father from work and were marking time. He was the postman assigned to deliver the mail to the many little communities around Cardston, such as Leavitt, Mountain View, Glenwood, and Hillspring. But today George would be home early because it was Christmas Eve. It was tradition for him to set up the Christmas tree as soon as he arrived. In preparation the children had been stringing mountains of popcorn and cutting out beautiful little paper stars to hang on the tree. They helped their mother put the precious colored candles in the tree clips, ready to clip onto the strongest branches.

Just as anticipated, George arrived home early from work,

happy to have the mail delivered for the day. He was tired and so cold he ached all over. But the overwhelming love from his family soon warmed his body and his soul. How he loved Christmas! With the help of Sidney and Rex, he soon hammered the cross planks securely to the bottom of the tree and set it up in the living room. Even without the decorations, it looked splendid!

As the children decorated, George silently ushered his wife into the kitchen away from the happy bedlam. George was troubled. He shared with Ingeborg the final events of his workday. As he was heading home, he had been informed of a late train delivery of ten crates to the station. These crates were all for one family living in Hillspring. However, as it was so late in the day and almost dark, it was decided that the crates would have to wait until the day after Christmas for delivery. It was just too far to Hillspring, especially with the current blizzard conditions.

Every day for a week this family's father had come to the train station to check the arrival of any packages sent by their family in the United States. All George knew about this Hillspring family was that they had several children and were experiencing very hard times. Christmas Eve had brought this Mr. Jeppson back to the Cardston station for one final, desperate check for the crates. He had left empty-handed and devastated. Apparently, the Jeppsons had written to their relatives asking to send anything they could for Christmas, perhaps some old quilts to keep them warm or a little money to buy coal.

George and Ingeborg were deeply religious and had great faith. Quietly they knelt and prayed for direction. After the prayer they looked into each other's eyes and knew what had to be done. Those crates needed to be delivered that night! But Ingeborg had one firm request: George must take Sidney, the oldest son. George had sight in only one eye due to an affliction suffered early in their marriage. With his limited eyesight, daylight deliveries were no problem, but nighttime perception would be a tremendous challenge, especially in blizzard conditions.

So George summoned Sidney and quietly explained the situation. Sidney did not hesitate a second. While they prepared to leave, the other children were informed of the impending trip. They pitched in with preparations like making sandwiches and filling thermoses. The little ones stuffed their father's pockets with nuts and candies for nibbling during the journey. All were secretly worried and saddened that their family would be apart on Christmas.

After the sleigh was hitched up, the family gathered to pray. Then with great faith they watched the sleigh quickly disappear into the snowy night. In no time at all, George and Sidney arrived at the station, loaded the crates, and set off for Hillspring. With hot rocks at their feet for warmth and scarves wrapped around their faces, they braved the blizzard that Christmas Eve.

Back home, as the blizzard raged on, the children hung their stockings, said their prayers, and scurried off to bed, hoping to see their father and brother by early Christmas morning. Meanwhile, the sleigh journey continued through the night. It took a total of eight hours to reach the Jeppsons' home. Many times during the trip, the Schows had felt special guidance and a sense of peace that they would reach their destination safely. They were relieved to see a light on at the Jeppson house when they arrived. It was the early hours of Christmas morning, and George knocked quietly. He must have looked quite a sight as the snow had turned to ice from his breath, creating frozen icicles that hung from his scarf around his face.

The woman exclaimed at the sight in front of her when she opened the door. George explained their purpose for coming, and the crates were unloaded into the house. It was obvious from the bare and humble surroundings that the Jeppsons would have had no Christmas without this delivery. They watched Mrs. Jeppson's eyes sparkle as they helped her unload the new quilts, mittens, shoes, coats, and other clothes for the children. There were hams and bacon, fruit, jam, and candy of every kind. They unloaded flour and sugar, nuts and spices, even small toys for the children. There was a note included telling the Jeppsons that the whole surrounding valley in Idaho had held bazaars to donate these items to the family. A humble request for some old quilts had turned into an abundance of love and sustenance from hundreds of caring people. George and Sidney left a very happy and deeply grateful Mrs. Jeppson and started the long trip home. With warm rocks at their feet and a lightened load on their sleigh, they drove off.

As the sun rose over the Schow home, the children rushed to check on their stockings and to see if their father and brother were home. The children took up a vigil at the window to await their return. Finally, just after lunch, Paul spied the familiar sleigh and everyone came running. Exhausted but happy, George and Sidney stumbled into the house and into the arms of their loved ones. They told of the Jeppson family and how essential the crates and contents were, not only for Christmas, but also to the family's survival through the winter. They told how they felt God had guided and protected them on the long journey. Tears of love and gratitude filled George's eyes as he held his family close. They were indeed blessed. George tried to imagine the joy and happiness in the Jeppson family that Christmas morning. This "special delivery" Christmas miracle would never be forgotten in the Jeppson or the Schow family households.

—GAYLA WOOLF HOLT
Cardston, Alberta, Canada

The Long Trek Home

OR SEVERAL YEARS, my family traveled to Steamboat Springs in the mountains of Colorado to spend the Christmas holidays with my wife, Jill, and me. We would snowboard, ski, and snowmobile along with the rest of the town. We would also celebrate my dad's Christmas Eve birthday.

Christmas Eve day, 1996, dawned like any other. My brother, Greg, my brother-in-law, Patrick, and I took the snowmobile and our snowboards up to Buffalo Pass. Patrick dropped us off and rode down to the pickup spot where we were to meet him after our run. It was a great day with fresh snow, which, in my case, leads to a loss of IQ. Even though I had lived in the mountains for four or five years and had been in this area before, my adrenaline was really pumping. I think I had also started to lose my respect for Mother Nature—not a very smart thing to do. The first time you go out in the mountains by yourself, you know you've got to find your way back, so you really pay attention. After a while, you grow complacent.

We had snowboarded all day, and I was tired. I knew I was farther to one side of the mountain than I wanted to be, but I thought I could drop down and get to the pickup place that way. I was having a blast.

Greg said the last he heard of me was a big "Yeehaw!" as I went over the ridge. I was coming around the corner when the snow started rolling under me—a mini avalanche! I rode it as far as I could, fast. The next thing I knew, I was in a creek bed. This was not in the game plan at all. Creek beds are dangerous places, especially when they're covered with snow, because the snow and ice crust could break at any moment and plunge me into the water. I had no sense of direction, no idea where I was. I decided to follow the creek bed around to see where it would lead. But the snow was waist deep and it was difficult to maneuver. Still, I eventually went about five miles.

After a while the sun set, and a dark, foreboding sky enveloped me. I knew I was in a dangerous situation; I needed to regroup and think things out before my condition became even more life-threatening. About four feet below me lay the creek. If I got wet, I would be in real trouble. I was already sweating profusely, so I peeled off some of the layers so I would have dry clothes to wear later.

I kept telling myself not to panic. I felt as though there was a little guy on one of my shoulders flipping out, and a guy on the other shoulder staying calm and telling the other one to settle down. I knew at this point I could be either my own best friend or my own worst enemy. I knew I was physically strong enough to survive a night outside as long as I didn't get into any more trouble. The frustrating part was not being able to see; I had no idea if I had three more yards or three more miles to go. Still, I felt positive because I was confident I could survive. I remembered the previous Christmas Eve, when I had helped rescue a woman with a broken leg. Surely God wouldn't let me die after I had helped save someone else?

I had almost left my snowboard behind when I started walking, but decided to take it at the last minute. It was brand new and I couldn't bear the thought of leaving it behind. It turned out to be my saving grace. By jamming the snowboard into the deep snow, I was able to pull myself out of the creek bed and up onto the ridge. Without the board, I wouldn't have made it.

Once on the ridge, I knew the general direction I wanted to go, yet I had no way to see the route out. I had to zigzag my way up and down the mountain with my snowboard in the complete darkness while doing my best to avoid the trees around me. I was in an area unknown to me and by now it had been a good eight hours since the mini avalanche. I was tired and hungry. The darkness was everywhere—no moon, no stars, nothing. What a dismal and frightening way to spend my dad's birthday and Christmas Eve!

Then, as I started the ascent to the last ridge, the heavens opened and the brightest, fullest, highest moon appeared out of nowhere. Where there had been darkness there now shone the most brilliant light, illuminating my way out. And there, just ahead of me, I saw it: the road home. I learned later that the moon that night was as high as it ever gets, and that the last full moon on Christmas Eve had been in

1950. The next one wouldn't come until the year 2072. Mother Nature had forgiven my cockiness and blown away the clouds to light my path home.

Now it was easy to see where to go, and I spied a road amid the trees ahead—Spring Creek Trail. Though it was twisty and made for mountain bikers, I knew it would take me the remaining miles back to Steamboat. I made a short-cut from the road but ended up in a drainage ditch up to my shoulders in snow. Oh yeah, I was making good decisions now! By then I was exhausted and getting fed up, and I started swearing out loud for the owls to hear.

All of a sudden I heard someone say, "Chris?" It was a woman's voice. "Jill?" I said, incredulously. Was I hallucinating? No, it was not Jill, but thankfully, it was the Search and Rescue team, on their way to find me. It was four-thirty in the morning Christmas Day, and one of the first people to reach me was the husband of the woman I had helped rescue the previous Christmas Eve. When word spread around town that I was missing, he had sworn to my wife that he wouldn't leave me out there, no matter how long it took to find me. Meeting him one year later renewed my faith that God had not abandoned me on that lonely mountaintop in Steamboat Springs. He had given me a glorious Christmas moon to light my way home.

"And there appeared a great wonder in heaven: a woman clothed with the sun, and the moon under her feet..." (Rev. 12:1).

—CHRIS STEBBINS
Steamboat Springs, Colorado

The Day the Curtains Came Down

HEY CAME TO Sweden like a flock of weather-driven migrant birds and took ground in our little town. We first saw them in church. One after the other they entered, lit a candle, and genuflected, the flickering candlelight reflected in their dark brown eyes as they crossed themselves.

The family filled almost a whole pew: there was the mother at one end, then a row of nine children, all with bluish-black hair like their parents. At the other end of the long line sat the father, holding the baby of the family in his arms. They stood out against the rest of the congregation like exotic birds in a flock of pigeons. Many of us glanced at them now and then, wondering who they were.

Our curiosity was satisfied the next day when we found the dark-eyed family smiling at us from the front page of our local newspaper. Underneath we read their story: The family came from Syria, where they belonged to the Christian minority. They had come to Sweden because they had relatives here and had applied to the Swedish immigration authorities for permission to stay in the country permanently. They did not anticipate any difficulties, as they already had relatives in the country.

The immigration authorities were renowned for taking their time with applications of this kind. In this case they were extremely slow in making their decision and the uncertainty about the outcome caused a great deal of anxiety within the family. Their situation was discussed in the newspaper and people in our little town took a lively interest in it. Whenever a few people met in shops, someone would take up the subject: What would happen to this large family?

At last—big, black letters on the front page: NO PERMIT TO STAY FOR THE ASSYRIAN FAMILY. We had suspected this would happen, but all the same, after seeing the family for so long and after getting used to having them around, we had all somehow begun to believe that in this particular case the authorities would make an exception. They could not possibly turn this family out of the country, even though they had entered illegally. The news really shook up the whole town.

Immediately after the decision the police had gone straight to the family's apartment to collect them, but the family was gone. No one had seen or heard them leave. People in the town, including the police, suspected that the minister of our church might have had something to do with their disappearance, but no one uttered that notion, and the police did not question him.

The family remained in hiding. They were split into small

groups as they dared not take the risk of being caught. All they could do was hope and wait. One night at the end of November, the minister called my husband and me. "The three oldest Assyrian children cannot stay where they are and there is no place for them to go. Can you take them?"

We live only three miles outside our little town. Hiding them in our home was not going to be easy. There was not anyone in the area, child or adult, who would not recognize them. But we hesitated for only a second and then said yes. That night we put up curtains on our windows.

My husband Olle and I decided that all we could do was use common sense and try to make the children's lives as normal as possible. And a normal life for children meant school. So I went to their school and asked the teachers for their books and other school things. "Just in case I happen to run across someone who knows where those children are . . ." I explained rather vaguely. I got the materials, no questions asked.

The next day the minister arrived late in the evening with Mary, fourteen, Magdalena, eleven, and little Eliah, eight years old. They were tense and scared but we welcomed them with open arms. And then we began the normal life. I told the children that they would have to take up their schoolwork again or they would not be able to catch up with their classes. They stared at me as if they had not understood me. "School?" Mary said. "Can we have school again? Real school?"

"Of course you can," I said. "One day you will return to school and you must prepare for that."

"But what about our schoolbooks?" Mary asked. I emptied my bag over the table. Out fell schoolbooks, crayons, exercise books, pencils, erasers, and drawing pads. Their faces glowed with excitement.

"You need to be outdoors, too," I said. "But you have your school assignments to do. I am afraid you cannot go out until late in the evening." Mary gave me a glance that told me that she understood the real reason why they would have to stay indoors during the daytime: their dark eyes and dark hair would make them too easy to recognize. So they had better put off their outdoor activities until after dark.

Every night the children rode our horses in darkness or moonlight. They got a lot of fresh air and finally began to laugh again. Christmas was approaching, and one day I said, "What are you going to give your family for Christmas? Wherever you will spend Christmas, the others in your family will be thrilled to get something from you. And they will love presents that you have made yourselves more than anything you can buy."

My husband and I went through our closets and found things that had been long forgotten by our family—pieces of scrap leather, balls of wool, ribbons, buttons, plastic pearls, cardboard boxes, and so on. The children's imagination set to work immediately as we dumped the stuff on the table in front of them. What discussions, what thoughtful frowns, what excited plans! They began to make their gifts with great enthusiasm, and the days seemed far too short for them, what with the lessons, horseback riding, and gift making. Eliah decided to knit a potholder for his mother. Wherever he went he dragged his ball of wool behind him on the floor while his knitting needles went click, click, click in his little hands. The artistic Magdalena made a colorful picture on a piece of cardboard, on which she glued pieces of cloth and leather. Mary made several little things, sewing neatly and quickly.

As Christmas drew closer all of us felt pretty safe and grew more careless. We decided to let the children accompany our children to a traditional Swedish holiday event, the celebration of Saint Lucia on December 13. Hopefully no one would recognize them if we tucked their black hair into their woolen hats. After all, it was going to be dark.

It was cold and dark and the snow was deep. They all looked delightful when they set out that evening. We had wound a string of glittering tinsel around their woolen hats and around their waists and they all carried a lit candle except my daughter, who had to lead the Shetland pony on which Eliah was riding. The children's eyes were like stars and the Lord himself must have enjoyed the sight, as they slowly walked away in the darkness.

Late in the afternoon on the following day there was a knock at the door. The children slipped upstairs as they always did and I opened the door. There stood a woman from one of the houses where the children had been singing Christmas carols. She was carrying a huge box in her arms. I invited her in and she stepped into the kitchen and set the heavy box on the table, pretending not to see the mess of schoolbooks scattered all over it. With a completely blank face she said, "I understand you have guests."

"Well, yes," I said. "We have some little relatives here. . . ."

"Relatives, yes, of course," she said. " So I thought I would bring a few things that might come in handy. I mean, it does cost extra to have visitors. Even if they are relatives. And I happened to have a few things at home that we do not need." She knew, I thought. God bless her, she knew and wanted to give us a hand! She would not tell anyone.

In the box I found canned fruits, vegetables, cornflakes, cookies, frozen fish, and a huge smoked leg of moose. There was enough food to last us until Christmas. We could not say a word—but our hearts felt as light as balloons as we put all of the food away.

Christmas was now just days away. We had expected to receive a message of some kind, news about the rest of the family. But there was not a word from anyone. In the afternoon on Christmas Eve the children finished making the last of the presents. There was nothing more for them to do. We all sat down at the table for cups of hot cocoa and coffee. We did not talk much. We just sat there. There *had* to be a message for them before Christmas!

Suddenly the telephone rang. It was the minister. "Turn on the radio!" he said. "The immigration authorities have changed their decision—the family has been given permission to stay permanently in Sweden! It is a miracle!" It was a blessed evening, indeed.

The last we saw of our three little stowaways were the children's hands eagerly waving good-bye in the back window of the minister's car as it disappeared down our little road. And on Christmas Day, with thankful hearts, we took down the curtains.

—KERSTIN BACKMAN
Grängesberg, Sweden

A Teacher's Christmas Tradition

INCE CHRISTMAS 1971, it has been my private holiday tradition to reflect upon a small tattered box and its precious contents, to remind me of the true meaning of giving and unselfish love.

While I was student teaching during that fall, I was assigned the responsibility of working closely with a "difficult" seven-year-old who had been neglected in so many ways for all of those seven years. Raising two children of my own and believing I had the inside scoop on kids, I accepted the challenge with enthusiasm. I could see that this boy had the potential to succeed, but as too frequently happens, his failure to conform to any social or academic criterion had gained him the reputation of being troublesome at school.

To my dismay, the task of getting through to and working with the boy was much harder than I'd ever imagined. I was repeatedly discouraged as I was hit, cursed at, and spat upon by this tiny ragged imp who was so emotionally starved that he was unable to accept any form of understanding or caring. Over the weeks, however, my unrelenting efforts and patience finally began to be rewarded, and the little boy slowly started showing improvement—physically, emotionally, and academically. As we bonded, his truancy lessened and he started to make friends and participate in group activities.

A few weeks into our newfound trust, the boy confided in me a pending trade with a classmate: my little guy was going to trade his only pair of gloves (which I had previously given him for his often-cold hands) for a red plastic shoe bag with a drawstring. Today, these types of bags are commonplace, but in the early seventies they were just making their appearance, and my boy was completely enamored with the shiny bright-red bag. The trade was made.

With not much to call his own, the boy became obsessed with his new prized possession. For many weeks, discussions and written work centered around his wonderful plastic bag—its purposes, value, and beauty in his eyes. He was extremely protective of the bag, and he guarded it with a vengeance.

A month flew by. Christmas was coming and my semester's work was drawing to a close. On my last day, the children held a combination Christmas and going-away party for me. While saying my good-byes and opening presents the children had bought me, I glanced up to see my boy abruptly leave his seat, and then the room. For a fleeting moment I entertained thoughts of having lost him, after all we had been through. But shortly thereafter, another teacher returned him to our room, after he was found in her classroom searching the wastebasket and asking for a rubber band.

With one small hand held behind him, he quietly approached my desk and slipped something under the rest of the gifts.

I continued opening the remaining trinkets, giving hugs and thank-yous. Finally I came upon a tiny, torn, faded green box wound with a rubber band. As I slipped the band from the box, my eyes briefly met the boy's. His smudged little face was glowing with an ear-to-ear smile. Folded carefully in the box was his treasure, the red plastic bag. My throat tightened and my eyes started to burn, but my heart was warmed and so touched by the extraordinary love he had shown me with his special gift.

This December, I will again celebrate Christmas with my own twenty-seven-year tradition: I will peek at the tattered green box holding the old red plastic bag as it lay tucked away in its secret place, holding for me the true meaning of giving. As it was for that young boy, the bag is my prized possession.

—KAREN MORROW
Kalamazoo, Michigan

Foggy Day

T WAS NOT the best of Christmas seasons that year, 1944. As I rode down through California's Central Valley on the train on December 23, I had plenty of time to think about my husband Ed, in the Air Force, loading bombs onto planes at the Battle of the Bulge. Although he had been diligent about writing two or three times a week until now, it had been weeks since I'd last heard from him. I dreaded the news that might be slowly winding its way toward me.

The usually dependable Southern Pacific train was anything but dependable during wartime. As the hours wore on I realized that although the schedule called for the train to arrive in Tulare at 11:00 P.M., we were not going to arrive at eleven or twelve or even at 1:00 A.M. Finally, at three in the morning, the train pulled into the station. The depot had long since closed for the night, and I looked anxiously around for signs that someone had come to meet me. As a schoolteacher living up north in Sacramento I made this train trip home quite regularly and my folks always came to the station to pick me up. But that morning there was no sign of them.

"Louise!" I heard someone calling my name from the parking lot. Peering out into the thick tule fog peculiar to the valley, I could make out a lone car. To my surprise I saw that it was not my parents emerging from the fog, but two old pals from high school who had been sitting there in the cold and dark for hours waiting for my train to arrive. They were tired and worn not only from the long wait, but also from the yearly ritual that orange growers undergo in cold weather to keep their trees from freezing—lighting smudge pots in the orchards to create a low, heavy smoke to keep the warmth close to the ground. Growers' children would sometimes drag into school in the morning with rings under their eyes from smudging all night and black streaks on their faces from the oily smoke.

I was overjoyed to see them, but I wondered where my parents were. As we drove through the countryside toward my hometown of Strathmore, they filled me in on my family's news: My grandmother had broken her hip and was in the hospital. My sister Barbara, due to give birth to her first child, was in the same hospital with what appeared to be serious complications with her baby. An X ray showed a breech baby with an abnormally large head. The doctor feared the worst. My father had been close to a breakdown and was lying in bed with worry.

Adding this distressing information to the worry I already had about my husband, I thanked my friends for the ride and went into the house to see what I could do to help. I found my sister's best friend close to hysterics. Like mine, her husband was also at the Battle of the Bulge. He was a doctor stationed at Nancy, and she had not heard from him in weeks, either. But the immediate problem at hand was to track down Barbara's husband, Giz, to tell him of the latest development with his wife's pregnancy. The two of us turned our attention from worrying about our own husbands to worrying about Barbara's. He was a B-24 pilot due to head out to fight in the Pacific, and we found that he was currently only three hundred miles to the north of us, on an air base in San Francisco. His commanding officer told us that he was on alert status and ready to be shipped out to the Pacific at any time. He would not be able to attend the birth.

December 24 passed slowly. We went back and forth to the hospital all day long, listening all the while to the terrifying news on the radio about the fight raging in Europe. As the day wore on, we were told that the doctors did not want to delay Barbara's delivery any longer, and that they planned to do a cesarean. Good news arrived when another set of doctors at the other end of the hospital told us that Grandmother was doing much better. And then suddenly, standing before us, bleary-eyed, his uniform rumpled, was Barbara's husband.

In a foolhardy split-second decision, Giz had decided to go AWOL the minute he'd heard of his wife's condition. If a baby was about to be born, he was determined to be there, despite how the Air Force felt about it. Hitchhiking on Highway 99, he'd caught ride after ride from sympathetic drivers all too willing to stop and help a serviceman. After a dozen or so different rides, he arrived in town and made his way to the hospital.

Barbara was overjoyed to hear that her husband was at hand, and the beautiful, perfectly normal baby boy was born without incident.

We spent a joyous night that Christmas Eve. My father got out of bed in great spirits to begin the holiday celebrations. With our Christmas looking brighter, we turned our attention to the next problem—getting Giz back to San Francisco before the Air Force noticed he was gone.

Gas was a precious commodity during the war, and none of us had enough gas coupons to last the long drive up through the valley to San Francisco. Hitchhiking slowly back on Christmas Day was his only option.

I drove Giz out to the road to begin his journey back that morning. As I made my way through orange groves along the country road toward the main highway, the gray tule fog was so thick I could hardly see the front end of my own car. Oh Lord, I thought to myself, how will Giz ever be able to pick up a ride in this fog? In his beige uniform no one would be able to see him standing by the side of the road.

But when I let him out of the car a battered black farm truck stopped almost immediately. Sizing up the driver as one of the local farmers out to make an early morning delivery, I felt even more discouraged. "Giz will never make it to San Francisco at this rate. I'll bet that fellow is just going up the road to the next ranch."

It turned out that the local farmer wasn't headed for his ranch. He was on his way up to San Francisco on business, with enough gas coupons in his wallet to take him the whole way. The farmer dropped Giz off a few blocks from the bar-racks. Giz slipped in with a few other fellows on their way back from Christmas services, and no one was ever the wiser about his absence from the field to attend his son's birth.

The letters started arriving from France the next week.

—LOUISE REARDON
Sacramento, California

The Bride Doll

OM AND DAD told all five of us children to "stay in the car!" as they ran across the street and stood helpless in front of our burning business. Their silhouettes looked small and frail in the darkness of the night, against the flames and smoke, the flashing police lights, and the spray of water from the fire truck. We hung out of every window of the station wagon on that cold late November night. We watched for hours, but time somehow stood still. Finally, as the flames died down, our parents took us home.

The next morning the smell of smoke lingering in our clothes and hair reminded us of the night's catastrophe. Dad had already left to see what could be salvaged from the business. We coaxed Mom into taking us down to see what remained. Nothing. The entire building had burned to the ground, taking with it cash, office records, furniture, supplies, tools, inventory, and two little kittens of a litter of six who had made their home in the business. The mother cat's burned tail and feet told the story of a valiant rescue when we found the remaining four kittens, singed but alive, in the alley.

Our faces became smudged with soot and ash. The only clean part was where the trail of tears had trickled down our cheeks. I thought my parents' tears, like mine, were for the lost kittens. Only when I grew up did I come to understand the desperate circumstances our family was now in. We were uninsured, yet my father was responsible for the contents of the building. Collectors were soon at our door; our family was in financial ruin.

Christmas was less than a month away. The excitement of the season soon swept me away from the charred ash of our circumstances. In my innocence, my mind turned to presents. I had wanted a bride doll for Christmas, just like the one my dear friend had. The doll was beautiful, with a white lace dress and veil and a pearl necklace. I had written countless notes to Santa describing her in every detail. I spoke of her day and night. Youth shielded me from the deep sorrow in my parents' hearts, as they knew they simply couldn't afford such an extravagance.

Then one day my mother sat down at her sewing machine and began to cut pieces of material from my dad's good white shirt. I loved watching my mother create at her machine. Those were times of heart-to-heart talks of shared hopes and dreams. As the white pieces began to take shape, I could tell that it was a doll dress. Of course, I thought it was for me, but Mother quickly told me that a man had asked her to make a doll dress for his little daughter for Christmas. It was the only gift she was to receive, so my mother worked hard to give it her best. For days I watched my mother sew the dress and then the veil. I was surprised as Mother cut into her white lace jacket that went with her beautiful black dress, and as she opened the pearl buttons she had been saving. Then she cut the ribbon off her favorite dress—all to create the most gorgeous bride doll gown and veil I had ever seen. I began to hint to her again, but her firmness stuck: It was not for me.

The day came when Mother asked to borrow my baby doll, the one I never let go of, to see if the dress would fit it. Apparently, the little girl for whom the dress was intended had a doll just like mine. It was a perfect fit. But as quickly as the dress was on my doll, it was whipped off. Mother borrowed my doll once more as she carefully untied the clasp of her own pearl necklace and measured off just enough pearls to make a doll's necklace.

The next day, the white thread in the sewing machine was replaced with red. The doll's gown was gone. Red, blue, and yellow fabric that would become Superman suits for my three young brothers replaced the lace and ribbon. I rushed to change my letter to Santa. I wanted a dress exactly like the one my mother had just made. I stood beside the machine and asked her how to spell "instead" and then asked her if ten "reallys" were enough to let Santa know I had changed my mind and really wanted what she had made. She smiled and wiped the tears from her eyes and assured me that ten "reallys" were probably enough.

On Christmas morning the cry went out from my older

brother: "Everyone up, it's Christmas!" We scrambled from our beds into the living room. Right there, beneath the tree, sat my baby doll dressed in a gown and veil exactly like the one Mother had made. I was so excited! I ran to hug my parents who sat holding hands on the sofa. My brothers had already shed their pajamas and jumped into their Superman outfits. Amid the chaos, I knelt down and looked with amazement at my beautiful bride doll. I made my way back to my parents and nuzzled in between them. I showed them every detail of the gown and veil and how perfectly the necklace fit. I made my parents laugh and cry when I said it wasn't quite as nice as the one my mother had made, but that the little girl deserved it because she was getting only one gift for Christmas. I was unaware, as I felt I had everything, that I had only one gift also.

My mother's gift only got better with time. The fabric and lace became old and worn after so much love and attention, but the bride doll never lost its magic for me. Some of the beads were lost along the way, but I continued to cherish my doll year after year.

Now, more than thirty-five years later, my mother's gift is brighter and more meaningful than ever as I recall the vision of my dad wearing an older white shirt that year so that his newer one could be used to make my bride doll. I think of my mother's Sunday dress without its lace jacket and of another dress without its decorative ribbon. And I will never forget the image of her pearl necklace, still a treasure to her, but worn just a few inches shorter.

For me the great miracle of Christmas lies in the gift of

self—the only gift that truly endures. It began with the first Christmas and God's gift to us of his Son. Perhaps, then, this is why at Christmastime we look a little deeper into our hearts to find the gift only we can give—the gift of love.

—VALERIE HOYBJERG
American Falls, Idaho

The Healing Power
of Prayer

T WAS CHRISTMAS and my husband and I were both tired. We had turned in our grades for fall semester at the university where we taught and had packed up our children and suitcases for a trek to Grandma and Grandpa's house in sunny California. David, my husband, nicked his finger while he was zipping up the suitcase, but it didn't bleed and he paid no attention to it. Just as we were leaving, my father called and said his mother had just passed away. Her funeral would be right after Christmas.

On Christmas Eve, David mentioned he felt sore under his arm, but thought it would go away. The next day we sat around opening gifts with our children and everyone else who had gathered for the funeral. As we finished the last present, David suddenly started shaking and had to lie down. Over the next two days David got progressively worse. His body started aching, especially his arm, and he could hardly stand the pain. He could hold no food down. I called our doctor in Utah, and he said it sounded like the flu, so when Tuesday morning came, I felt we could leave David for an hour while we went to the church for Grandma's funeral. After all, I was one of the speakers, and David could take care of himself for a little while.

The funeral was a warm reunion of all of my relatives. I am the oldest granddaughter, so I spoke representing all the female cousins. Grandma was ninety-four and lived a long, productive life, so I spoke about Waite women being strong women. As I sat down, a neighbor gave me a note that had been sent to the church: my husband had been taken by ambulance to the hospital.

When I arrived, I found David on the brink of death. He was barely coherent, but coherent enough to be in a lot of pain. Between his unbearable body aches he told me that shortly after we left for the funeral, he could feel his body starting to shut down. He felt a voice warning him, "You need an ambulance now." After feeling this voice several times, he crawled to the phone and dialed 911. The operator tried to keep him alert and talking, but in the end, David hung up, crawled to the front door to unlock it, and lay down on the couch. The paramedics found him barely conscious with no detectable pulse, so they rushed him to the hospital.

After many tests, including X rays and ultrasounds, the doctors were baffled; they couldn't diagnose his problem. When David emerged from an MRI, he had a large purplish-black spot on his side. "Was he drunk in an alley last night? Did someone kick him?" they inquired. I assured them that was not the case. After a few more minutes of conferring with each other, the doctors pulled me aside.

"We think we know what this is. It may be necrotizing fasciitis, popularly known as flesh-eating bacteria. Have you heard of it?"

"I don't pay much attention to tabloid diseases," I replied.

"This is a virulent bacterium. We are going to take him into surgery and cut him from wrist to hip, looking for infected tissue. This is a very rare disease. The bacteria probably entered his body in a cut. Has he cut his finger or arm lately?"

"He nicked his finger zipping up the suitcase, that's all."

"This bacterium is common, but our body usually fights it off. For some reason it has attacked your husband. He has a five to ten percent chance of living through this—it is that serious—and he will probably look like a shark bit him when we are finished."

I knew that a 5 to 10 percent chance of living was a kind way of saying my husband was probably going to die. "I say a ten percent chance is worth going for. Let's go for life. Let's save him," I replied. All the children came into the room to wish their father well, and then, in the hall, the nurses brought us chairs and juice so we wouldn't faint. We were all in shock that our completely healthy husband/father was close to death with a devastating disease. Right before they wheeled him away I leaned over my semicoherent husband and whispered, "Choose life, David. Choose life."

I also knew how to increase the odds. I gathered my family into the surgery waiting room, and since it was empty, we knelt and prayed together. I said, "Heavenly Father, the doctors don't know what is wrong with David, but You know. They don't know how to heal him, but You know. Please bless them that they will figure out how to save David's body. If it be Thy will." The last phrase was hard to say, but necessary, because I don't command God.

Then I went into a deserted office and, with the hospital's permission, made some long-distance calls: to David's parents, the pastor of our church congregation, my good friend Beth, and the English department chair at the university. I asked each person to please call everyone we knew and ask them to pray for David: "The next two hours decide my husband's life. Please pray for him. I believe in miracles and I believe in prayer." By the end of the day, hundreds of our friends were praying for David.

The surgeons emerged several hours later with some good news. The bacteria had not spread as far as they thought, and David was still alive. We cheered and felt as though our prayers had been answered. But David was still extremely sick, still on the verge of death. He had a team of about twelve doctors, each with a different specialty. They told us that the strep A bacteria were destroying David's skin and underlying tissues and muscles. The infection was spreading as fast as an inch per hour. The doctors performed major surgery every day, cutting out dead or infected tissue and putting David in a hyperbaric chamber for several hours a day. The chamber was full of 100 percent oxygen, and they would put him under pressure to force the oxygen right to the cells. David stayed alive two more days.

But he wasn't improving. His main surgeon talked frankly

with me. "I don't have a good feeling about this," he warned. "I think the bacteria have gone to his neck and heart." I went home believing that David's death was imminent, and I needed to think about emotionally letting him go. That night I spent the entire night trying to pray for David's life and trying to pull myself out of an enclosing darkness. I went back to the hospital ready to say good-bye to David, if that seemed what God willed. Instead, I was surprised by the surgeon's news that David had taken a turn for the better. His body was beginning to fight the bacteria.

That afternoon the surgeon informed me that he was bringing in someone to amputate David's arm, since it had lost most of the skin and much of the muscle. "But David is a pianist," I protested. "Please remember, when you are in the operating room, he is a pianist." At home, we decided to pray especially for his arm, although I admit I have never prayed for a specific limb before. Every day for a week the surgeons went in ready to amputate his arm, and every time they decided to leave it because the arm had just barely enough healthy tissue. However, they had nicked the main nerve, so they figured that although David would have an arm, it would be lame.

A few days later, David could wiggle his fingers and move his hand. "Well, it looks like you will be able to move it, but playing the piano is doubtful and you'll have to give up tennis," his surgeon told him. "If you're able to get out on the courts at all, you'll play like an old man." David, eager just to get his life back, immediately challenged the surgeon to a game of tennis when he recovered.

David lived, but over the next few months, he lost nearly

50 percent of the skin on his upper body. The doctors replaced the skin with grafts from his thighs, until he was all covered in skin again. He eventually left the hospital and returned home to a major celebration. At home, once we were alone, David and I looked at each other and decided he should try the piano. I suggested that if he could play a few chords, I would define that as success. David apprehensively put his hands on the keyboard, not knowing what to expect. Would his fingers work? Was his dexterity gone for good? I didn't breathe. David started to play, and incredibly, he could still play the piano beautifully. He composed a piece on the spot.

But this is not the end. From that Christmas to the next, David went to physical therapy to regain flexibility in his chest, back, and arms. As the next Christmas came around, we decided again to visit my parents for the holidays, just to prove to ourselves that we could have a vacation with no one sick or in the hospital. David eagerly called his surgeon and reminded him of his earlier tennis challenge. The surgeon was delighted and on Christmas Eve, David and his doctor met at a tennis court and played doubles against another pair of doctors. David's surgeon cheered every time David hit the ball. He called the other doctors to the net to show them David's scars and the extensive skin grafts. By the end of the game, David and his surgeon had won, forty-love.

Although that year was extremely difficult for us, it was also a holy time. Through the love and prayers of hundreds around us, our family experienced three miracles: David lived, he kept his arms, and he can still play tennis and Beethoven sonatas.

And I find my prayers have become mostly prayers of thanks.

—DELYS WAITE COWLES
Provo, Utah

The Cabbage Patch Christmas

HRISTMAS IS TRULY a marvelous time of year. The warmth of love for fellowmen, the scent of evergreen and holly, and the touch of magic in the air all combine to create a stage for miracles. One such miracle touched our family thirteen or fourteen years ago . . . you remember, the year of Cabbage Patch mania.

What Beanie Babies are to children today, Cabbage Patch dolls were to kids in the 1980s. What was it about those chubby-cheeked dolls that grabbed the hearts of little girls around the country, not to mention their sentimental moms? Whatever it was, Coleco hit the nail squarely on the head, and the charge was on.

Their marketing efforts were right on target at the McKinnon family home in Winter Park, Florida. Three curly-headed girls—Courtney, Ashley, and Alexis—knew what they *needed* for Christmas. Cabbage Patch dolls topped each of their lists. Cabbage Patch was the topic of every secret club conversation and every bathtub rub.

It was heart-wrenching. However, it was not heart-wrenching enough to send me out in pursuit. There was simply too much else to be done. Remember the stories in the papers of mobs surging for the few dolls available, with all thoughts of Christmas cheer left in their empty shopping carts? Although the pictures of the dolls in catalogs and sales flyers had won my heart, I still was not prepared to "fight the good fight" to secure one. Besides, in our family, one doll would not do it. If there were to be Cabbage Patch dolls under the tree, there had to be three. It simply was impossible. No one could have the time or energy at this busy season to deliver the anxiously desired dolls.

Well, to the rescue rode Dad. Joel McKinnon is truly the personification of Father Christmas. No child's whim is too big to discourage this maker of marvelous Christmas memories. *His* girls would have a Cabbage Patch Christmas.

The big break came with a hot tip from a good friend. A shipment of Cabbage Patch dolls would be delivered to the Sanford, Florida, Kmart that Sunday morning. If Joel was there before 8:00 A.M., a place in line would be assured and then he was just a hop, skip, and a jump away from ownership of the elusive little cuties.

Armed with hiking boots for traction and his black-and-red hunting jacket for the illusion of strength, Joel headed north on Highway 17-92 at sunrise. Upon arrival, he was disappointed to learn that the hot tip had made the circuit. Almost one hundred shoppers were in line by eight, and the store did not even open for two hours.

His plan was further complicated by the fact that each customer was limited to two dolls. Fortunately, he could use the next two hours to become lifelong friends with the closest man in line, who needed only one doll. It must have been a laborious two hours . . . but in the end the bond was solidified and when the door opened, Joel and his new comrade headed for the mountain of dolls.

I will spare you all the humiliating details, but suffice it to say that it was one of the more nightmarish sixty minutes of Joel McKinnon's life. Yet, in the end, when the dolls were safely in his trunk and the comrade was rewarded adequately to release his grasp on his second doll (and Joel thought he had made a friend), he had the feeling of a job well done.

A safe hiding place was selected at home and Olivia, Shannon, and Norma Louise waited to meet their new mommies. On Christmas Eve, as we were working our midnight magic, I made out the Cabbage Patch gift tags: "To Courtney, from Santa"; "To Ashley, from Santa"; "To Alexis, from Santa." But as Joel passed me on his way to the shed for an appropriate assembly tool, he stopped long enough to let me know my labels were not acceptable.

By golly, he had gone through some pretty bad times to secure those dolls and he was not going to give all the credit (and adoration) to the man in the red suit. No siree. These dolls were from Daddy!

With new gift cards in place, Olivia and Shannon and Norma Louise were initiated into the McKinnon clan in the wee hours of Christmas morning. Our three daughters made darling, if somewhat rowdy, mothers. And amid all the ado, the Daddy of them all was beaming. Clearly the hours of misery in Sanford were worth it. The memory was indelibly engraved on all.

The real miracle occurred later that afternoon. As Joel and I sat exhausted, watching the Christmas wrappings go up in smoke, our six-year-old son Matt approached us quietly (unlike his sisters). His story was the most touching of all.

You see, he had accidentally stumbled upon the hidden Cabbage Patch dolls while looking for a misplaced Frisbee days before Christmas. Instead of telling the girls or us, he had kept this secret to himself.

"I thought those would be Santa presents for the girls," he said, "and, if the tags had said they were from Santa, it would mean there was really no Santa like the other kids say, because I had found the dolls before Christmas.

"But Daddy," Matt continued, "the dolls weren't from Santa, they were from you. So, Dad, do you know what that means? Do you?"

Oh yes, Matt, Daddy knew!

"That means there *is* a Santa. And Dad, that makes me really happy. Isn't Christmas great?"

Yes, Matt. Christmas really is great . . . and so is your miraculous Santa.

—GENEAN MCKINNON
Winter Park, Florida

The Touch of an Angel

HAT IS IT?'' I asked as I entered the kitchen and saw my dad sitting in a chair at the kitchen table, his gray head resting in his hands. It was Saturday and I had stopped by for a visit, as I'd done every Saturday since Mom's death a year ago. At the sound of my voice, he glanced up. "I need to see a doctor. I don't feel well."

"But Dad, Dr. Halloway's out of town," I said. "He told you at church last week he intended spending Christmas Day fishing."

One glance at my dad's ashen pallor and his mouth twisted in pain, and I knew he was right. He was not well. I reached for the phone and dialed the surgery number. I listened to the recorded response, then replaced the receiver. "It's Christmas, Dad, and the surgery's not open. I'll take you to the hospital emergency room at St. George's. You've probably eaten something that disagrees with you. In a couple of hours you'll be feeling better." I helped him out of the chair and led him toward the front door and the driveway, where I'd parked my car.

On the drive to the hospital, I tried to keep the conversation light, talking about my two boys' activities at school. Dad nodded in response, but I could see from the frown on his forehead that the pain had not subsided. Twenty minutes later I pulled into the emergency entrance of the local hospital. I parked the car, and together we walked into the hospital. For two hours I drank free coffee and exhausted the magazine supply on the wooden table in the waiting room area. With nothing left to do, I closed my eyes and began to think back to the last couple of visits that I'd made to Dad.

He'd seemed well at the time, although I remembered him coughing. When I suggested he get it checked out, he reminded me that it was allergy season and that he had enough allergy medicine to last a lifetime.

"Miss Riley," a deep voice said near my ear.

Startled, I opened my eyes and looked up into the face of Dr. Luther, one of the three family physicians at Dr. Halloway's practice. "We are trying to get in touch with Dr. Halloway. In the meantime, I wanted to let you know we've examined your dad and we need you to sign some papers."

"Papers?" I mumbled. Then I noticed two pieces of white paper in his hand.

"You have to give us permission to operate."

"Operate? But Dad just ate something that didn't agree with him," I said. "He doesn't need an operation."

"I'm afraid his stomach trouble is a little more serious than that," Dr. Luther said. More serious? My stomach lurched at the word "serious."

"The X ray shows a dark spot. I'd like to take a look," Dr. Luther said.

As I sat in the waiting room, I listened to the rustle of the nurses in their crisp white uniforms striding down the corridor and watched them disappear into a room. Minutes later they'd reappear and continue on their way. Every so often an announcement blared from the overhead PA system, breaking the silence.

Two hours later, I turned at the sound of footsteps approaching the waiting room. Hands in pockets, stethoscope around his neck, Dr. Luther entered and strode toward me. There was no smile on his face. A lump formed in the back of my throat. Maybe Dad hadn't made it, I thought. "He's okay, isn't he?" I blurted out.

"Miss Riley, your father is in intensive care. He'll be sleeping for the next couple of hours."

Intensive care? "But Doctor, he's going to be all right, isn't he?"

He wet his lips before speaking. "The next few hours will be crucial. We had to remove the lining of his stomach to remove the cancer . . . then his heart gave us a scare. How long has he had a heart condition?"

Cancer? Heart condition? "But Dad's never been ill," I said, unable to disguise my puzzlement. "He visited the doctor for his allergies, but I don't remember him ever being really ill." I couldn't control the thoughts running through my mind. How could this happen? And to my dad? "You did get the cancer? All of it?" I managed to ask.

Dr. Luther nodded. "We did. I'll be in to check on him later." I thanked him and headed for my dad's room. As I entered and made my way to the bed, a clock in the distance struck three. I gazed at the wizened white face of the man lying in the bed with tubes in his nose. My dad was only sixty, but the man in the bed looked ten years older. How had he aged that quickly without my noticing? I wondered. And what had happened to the fighter I once knew? There was no fight in the man in the bed before me. I touched the frail hand lying on the white coverlet. I could barely feel his pulse. Only the beep, beep of a heart monitor near his bedside broke the eerie silence.

Suddenly I felt a hot tear trickle down my cheek. If only I had told him the things I had been meaning to tell him over the past few years—how much I loved him; how I loved those times when as a small child I had sat on his knee and listened to nursery rhymes; how as a teenager, I had appreciated his help in solving those unsolvable math problems. Now, I realized I might not get an opportunity.

I lifted his hand to my cheek. It felt cool against my hot skin. "Dear God," I prayed, "give me the chance to say all the things I've been meaning to say, but never found the time." I let go of Dad's hand and dropped into a chair near the bed. For the next couple of hours I stared at his face, half expecting my dad to open his eyes and be my old dad once again.

Eventually, Nurse Sutton, the day nurse, crept in, her soft-soled white shoes squeaking on the polished floor. She inspected the chart, took my dad's pulse, wrote the information on the chart, and left the room. By six o'clock my dad had not shown any signs of waking. I began to panic. What if he never woke up? What if I never got to speak to him again? My stomach churned. I reached for my handkerchief and blew my nose.

"Are you all right?" a soft feminine voice said at my side. I turned and saw a china doll face with wisps of hair the color of sunflowers, under a white cap. She was dressed in a white uniform like Nurse Sutton but was without a name tag.

"Beg your pardon?" I said.

"I heard you crying," she said. "Can I help?"

"It's been three hours and my dad hasn't awakened. I don't think he wants to fight," I said. "It's not like him. He was always a fighter."

The nurse touched my arm. "He's resting before the big fight," she said. Then she walked to the bed. Her long fingers curled around my dad's wrist. She glanced at her watch. Minutes later a smile crossed her cherry lips. "That's better." She released his wrist.

"The big fight?" I asked, somewhat puzzled by her comment.

"Why sure," she said. "He's been through a lot but when he wakes up, he'll feel bad. You'll have to help him get over it. You must show him he's got a lot more living to do."

I nodded, staring back at my dad. There certainly was a lot more living for my dad to do. I turned to thank her, but the room was empty. I hurried to the door and peered out. There was no one in sight.

I returned to the bed and my chair, making a mental note to thank her when she returned.

Thirty minutes later Dr. Luther appeared and checked the chart at the foot of the bed. Then he peered at my dad and at the monitor. "Good. The color's coming back into his cheeks. And his heartbeat is getting stronger."

"So he's going to be all right?"

Dr. Luther glanced across at me. "We'll have to wait and see. I'll send the nurse in to check his pulse."

"But the nurse was just in," I said.

Dr. Luther scratched his head. "Funny! There's only one note recorded on the chart."

Just then Nurse Sutton entered. "I've come to take Mr. Riley's pulse."

Dr. Luther turned. "Don't you mean record the pulse you took a few minutes ago?"

"But Doctor," I interrupted, "I meant the other nurse."

Dr. Luther smiled at me. "Miss Riley, I think you need some rest. Nurse Sutton is the only day nurse assigned to the case. And the night nurse doesn't come on for another three hours."

Just then a grunt caught our attention. My dad's eyes fluttered open. They focused on my face. He smiled. "Where's that nurse again?" he whispered. "The one with the touch of an angel?" Then his eyes closed once again. The only sound in the room was the beep, beep, and beep of the heart monitor as my dad slept on.

—ROSEMARIE RILEY
Fresno, California

To Hope and Pray

 Y MOTHER WAS, to me, the greatest example of love, kindness, tenderness, and self-
sacrifice. She was the truest teacher of fairness that I have
ever known, and not a day goes by that I do not miss her
in my life.

I grew up in a home my parents bought just before I was
born. My childhood was filled with tiny moments of caring
and love—hot cocoa and cookies on a rainy afternoon,
warm smiles and a pat on the back whenever I needed one.
And when I grew up and moved to a house to start my
grown-up life, I didn't go far—just a few miles away. I hoped
that I would be able to share my parents' love with my own
children and give them the same feeling of safety and security I'd grown up with.

But as I drove through the rain one December afternoon
in 1989, all of that security seemed to be dissolving, washing

away with every raindrop that fell. My mother was dying of lung cancer.

Christmas was my mother's favorite time of year. Oh, she'd sometimes complain about the hectic season she was having, but our family tree was always carefully decorated with her prized crystal ornaments, and I knew she took great pride in having such a special tree.

"Please, God," I prayed as I drove though the rain that day, "please let my mother live through one more Christmas." I pulled into a crowded shopping mall parking lot. "I'm not ready to let her go and I need her here with me." My heart was not up to shopping for presents that day, but I selected a gift or two for my husband and daughter. I knew I shouldn't let my own feelings of impending loss and betrayal spoil the holiday for my family.

In the center of an aisle stood a large display of Christmas ornaments. I thought an ornament might be a cheerful gift for my mother, something that would reconnect her with her love for Christmas and give her some hope. Once again my thoughts took the form of prayers, and I prayed that the gift of a simple ornament would give her the hope to see this blessed day one more time. One ornament on the display stood out in particular. I was drawn to a beautiful satin and pearl-encrusted heart. I removed it from the display and walked over to the cash register, pleased with my choice. As I laid it on the counter, I turned it over. And there, outlined in seed pearls on the back of the ornament, was the word "hope."

I stared at the ornament in disbelief. This was surely a sign that my mother, too, would receive hope from my gift and was meant to survive long enough to share one more Christmas with us.

I rushed to her house with the ornament, so eager to give it to her and tell her the story that I didn't even stop to wrap it. Clutching the plastic bag to my chest, I breathlessly told her my story. I told her what the word "hope" meant to me. She smiled quietly as she listened to my tangled tale, and then carefully hung the glimmering ornament on the big Christmas tree that stood in the corner of the living room.

But her "hope" was not the same as mine. As Christmas grew closer, my mother began to tell me that her desire was to die before Christmas came. She feared being ill over the holiday and forever filling our future holidays with sorrow. I assured her that all my father, my daughter, and I wanted was for her to be with us one last Christmas, sick or well. But she was insistent. "I hope to die before Christmas."

And she did. On December 7 of that year, my mother passed away, ending her long struggle against cancer. I buried the satin and pearl ornament with her. She left me, her only daughter, not only saddened, but also confused.

Hadn't my prayers helped me find the "hope" ornament as a sign that she would survive through Christmas? What was the message of my little Christmas miracle?

As the months after her death passed, I slowly began to realize that, in the end, God in His wisdom had answered my mother's prayer, not mine.

—CANDY CHAND
Antelope, California

Going Home

ARRIVED EARLY in the morning at the San Diego railroad station and joined throngs of anxious holiday travelers laden with baggage and Christmas gifts. We all slowly climbed aboard the long, overbooked holiday train. Lines of military and civilian passengers pushed and shoved each other, scrambling for the remaining seats.

The giant train engine, puffing steam, was ready to pull the train across the United States. It would take an eternity—four days and four nights—to reach New York City. Still weak from malaria and hurting from my recent battle wounds, I was not looking forward to this long, boring trip.

I struggled down the coach aisle, carrying my U.S. Marine Corps sea bag. Panic set in as I neared the end of the car. It was the last car and all the seats looked occupied. My anxiety was interrupted by a loud voice: "Over here, Marine, and hurry up. I have a seat for you."

I hurried over and sat down next to a U.S. Navy sailor, and thanked him for the seat.

"Hi, mate! They call me 'Ski' because of my long Polish last name."

I replied, "Hi, mate. They call me Eddy Lee, because of my long Ukrainian name." We both grinned and clumsily shook left hands. My wounded right hand was in a sling, and his right arm was amputated, with his empty jumper sleeve pinned up at the shoulder.

When I saw the many U.S. Navy men and women struggling through the narrow aisle, I asked Ski why he, a navy man, had given me, a marine, this seat. Ski said, "Well, I saw your shoulder patch, your combat ribbons, and battle stars, and I knew that you and I fought in the same campaigns. You were on the land, and I was on the sea." He added, "I served aboard the U.S.S. *Chicago*, a cruiser named after my hometown. I lost my arm when we were torpedoed off the island you were fighting on."

The coach door shut abruptly, and the train conductor called out, "Last call for Salt Lake, Denver, Chicago, and New York City. All aboard!" The locomotive's loud steam whistle blew, then with the clang of its large bell, we started for home. In a few rumbling minutes we picked up speed. Soon, with a resounding roar, we were crossing southern California, heading east.

Ski and I were both proud of the U.S. Navy and Marine Corps, but we were bitter toward the military hospital we had just left. This hospital had an inefficient administrative system, and their medical staff was overworked and burned out. Four years of war and the continuous flow of casualties rotating through this facility had created a callous attitude. We were disenchanted with the negative treatment we had received from the military and the apathetic civilian world since our return to the United States. It was this type of poor management that put us rehabilitating servicemen on a crowded train rather than on an airplane. Ski and I agreed that we both had become atheists and cynics after three years of war.

This would be my fourth Christmas away from home, and the season always made me sad because of the many friends who had died in battle during the holiday. Our iron horse was traveling at maximum speed, but it seemed as if we were not moving fast enough across the great American desert. We passengers had too much time on our hands. We could sleep sitting up in our seats, stand in line for meals and washroom, or reminisce bittersweet battle memories with our train mates. Soon we all tried to sleep the time away.

The train stopped in Salt Lake City. The scenery was fabulous, but the cold, snow-capped mountains had us all putting on our overcoats. Our coach car never did get warm, and most of us were coming from the tropics via California, so we would not warm up for weeks. En route to Denver our train wound ever so slowly through many tunnels, around picturesque snow-covered mountains and valleys. I consoled myself with the idea that time was no longer important. What was my hurry? I would miss Christmas at home by a day. My parents had split up, and I had no home to go to. My girlfriend of four years had sent me a "Dear John" letter, saying she had waited too long for me to return and had found someone else. And worst of all, when I was well enough for duty, I could be sent back overseas to battle again.

We left Denver early Christmas Eve morning in a snow-storm. Our train's whistle blew often as we charged across the prairie states through a howling blizzard. By nightfall we were somewhere in Illinois. Our train slowed to a crawl due to poor visibility. Its mournful whistle wailed continuously as we passed many small towns. It was cold and getting colder in our passenger car. *Lord, will my luck ever change?* I silently said.

The train conductor entered our car and called out, "It's ten o'clock, two hours to Chicago. Next stop, Chicago!" He dimmed the lights and left. Most passengers became quiet or had fallen asleep.

Ski turned to me and said, "You know, I'm worried about my family meeting me at the Chicago station and seeing me like this. I asked my girl not to come. What should I do or say to them?"

"Act natural. They know about your arm. Try to be your-self. You all love one another, and I'll bet they will thank God that you made it home alive. It will all work out fine, you'll see. Now let's try and get some sleep."

Suddenly, the train made an unscheduled, metal-screeching stop. A few waking passengers muttered, "What's going on? Must be a milk or mail supply stop. This sure as hell isn't Chicago." Others looked out of their frosty win-dows and said, "This is nowhere." Most of them went back to sleep.

I looked out and could see only a small, dimly lit railroad station surrounded by huge snowdrifts and darkness. The door at the other end of the car opened, and in the dim light, I could barely see a small boy and a mature woman coming into our coach. They slowly walked up the aisle, apparently looking for a seat. The two strangers cautiously headed back toward my end of the car. I closed my eyes and tried to get back to sleep, wondering why the train was not moving. I was dozing off when I heard a noise in front of me. I slowly opened my eyes and saw the young boy, about eight or nine, standing in front of me, staring. The boy smiled. "Welcome home and merry Christmas, marine," he said. My grandmother and I would like to give you a gift and thank you for serving our country." The boy handed me a dollar bill and then shook my hand. The grandmother put her arm around me and said, "God bless you." Then they both smiled and said, "Merry Christmas and good-bye."

I was surprised and very moved. I said, "Thank you, thank you very much." I looked down to search in my sea bag for some sort of Christmas gift to give the boy in reciprocation. When I looked up, they were gone.

Our train whistle blew; we lunged forward and were rolling again. I quickly looked out my window and saw the boy and his grandmother leaving the dismal railroad station. I waved good-bye as they slipped into the darkness. They did not see me. I sat back in my seat bewildered, wondering what had just happened. Was it real? I queried Ski and two other soldiers sitting across from me if they too had seen a little boy and his grandmother. "No," they said, "we were sleeping." Ski added, "You must have been dreaming."

My mind raced with questions. Who were they? Why had they passed by all those other servicemen, including other marines, and then stopped in front of me? Maybe, with all the medication I was taking for pain and malaria, it just could have been a strange, nice dream.

It was two more hours to Chicago, and I decided to try to get some sleep. But before closing my eyes, I looked down at my left hand and tightly closed fist. I slowly opened it. There it was: a crumpled one-dollar bill. My hand held the gift the young boy had given me—proving it really had happened. I fell asleep with my precious gift tucked safely in my pocket and a pleasant feeling in my heart—the nicest feeling I had had in a very long time.

Not long after that, the conductor came into the car and yelled, "Next stop, Chicago, five minutes!" Passengers were removing their baggage from the overhead compartments. I helped Ski take down his sea bag. He was home. People were jostling in the aisles to disembark. The train slowed as we pulled into Chicago's Union Station. Ski and I exchanged emotional good-byes as the train came to a complete stop. The crowd of passengers left through both exit doors. I sat back, waiting to continue my odyssey of another thousand miles to New York City.

It was midnight, and it was Christmas. As I looked out the train window, I was surprised to see hundreds of people, young and old, choirs of many ethnic and racial backgrounds on the station platform, all holding candles and sheet music and singing carols. The people and the station were all decked out with the Christmas spirit and decorations. It was a bitter cold, snowy Chicago Christmas, but the holiday spirit was cheerful and warmed all our hearts. As I was enjoying the joyful singing, our train doors opened and the choirs of young people paraded in. Each singer carried a tray of food and drinks. Each tray held a complete Christmas dinner with a small gift on it. There were enough trays for everyone in the train.

We were no longer strangers; we all sang, ate, and celebrated together. It was the most beautiful, festive Christmas I had ever had. Our generous Chicago hosts cheerfully wished us a "Very merry Christmas and welcome home!"

This train odyssey and these unbelievably beautiful events changed my bitter feelings; I really felt I had made it home for Christmas. Many years later, as I was telling this story to my family at Christmastime, I pondered out loud, "Who was that little boy on the train and why did he and his grandmother choose me?" Our young niece was playing on the floor with her new Christmas toys. She had been listening quietly to my sentimental Christmas story and replied, "I know."

We all looked at her and said, "You know what?"

"I know who the little boy was and why he picked you. The little boy was God and He chose you because you were very, very sad and disappointed with everyone and everything. He wanted to make you happy again and welcome you home, and He did."

Throughout the years, I knew that a Christmas miracle had happened to me when I needed it most, during the war, on the train, and in Chicago.

—EDWARD ANDRUSKO
Boulder, Colorado

The Year I Almost
Missed Christmas

WO DAYS AFTER Christmas, I stared out my
kitchen window at the soul-chilling rain and
cheerless fog. Nothing had gone as I'd hoped this holiday
season. My father was fast losing hope in his battle with
cancer, and I'd personally suffered severe disappointments.
The tenants in our rental house hadn't paid rent in many
months, and while we didn't have the heart to evict them,
we weren't financially able to carry them much longer.

Worse yet, I had ahead of me another surgical operation,
scheduled for the first week of the new year. Operations had
been the story of my life. And for me, appointments with
the surgeon's scalpel would never end. I was constantly
growing tumors because of my illness, neurofibromatosis.
Suddenly, the thought of it all seemed too much. I was tired.
Was the constant daily struggle even worth it, I wondered?

I gazed out the window again at the deserted bird feeder.
Then, from somewhere in the recesses of my mind, came a

line from a poem, although I couldn't instantly place its author. The line was "And no birds sing." Short and stark, those four words. No birds sang in my backyard or in my life.

The brightness and glitter of my Christmas decorations mocked the ocean of gloom surrounding me. I'd lost the very hope and joy of Christmas, and of living. I plunged into eradicating every trace of Christmas, then kept on cleaning house in a frenzy of busyness. By six that evening, my whole body ached from fatigue. Still, I found no peace.

Then, I remembered I'd promised Miss Wilson, the dear neighbor who'd been such an important part of my growing-up years, that we would drive to see the Christmas lights that night. I hadn't visited her the entire holiday season and I couldn't let her down. At eighty-one, she lived alone and hardly got out of the house anymore, except to go to the doctor.

With packages in hand, I tapped on her front door, just as I'd done hundreds of times before. During my girlhood her house had seemed a magical kingdom. A tinge of expectancy swept over me, as if something wonderful was about to happen.

Once inside her living room, I sank down into the tapestry sofa and handed Miss Wilson a trio of presents. She smiled warmly, yet her coifed silver hair and pastel lamb's wool sweater failed to mask her own ailments—shortness of breath and painful arthritis. She handed me a shimmering gold package. "This is a little late for Christmas," she apologized, avoiding my eyes. "I got it from a mail-order catalog."

I tore open the wrapping. "It's a book on crafting holiday

wreaths!" I exclaimed. "Let's make some of these next Christmas—like the old times."

"I don't expect to be here next Christmas," she answered softly, as her slippered feet smoothed and ruffled the nap of the rose plush carpet.

Her words stopped me cold. Christmas without Miss Wilson?

"Of course you'll be here," I insisted. I drew in a shaky breath and forced a smile. "And we'll both feel better once we see those Christmas lights," I said, changing the subject. I flipped on the porch light, then took her arm and guided her down the steps and into the front seat of my car. "They say the lights in Stamford Park are fabulous this year. Why, cars were lined up for twenty minutes the other night," I jabbered. "And 'Winter Wonderland' over in Kentucky— you've never seen such a festival of lights."

"Honey, let's stick close to home," she urged.

Over and over, I silently pleaded, *Lord, if it's not too late, help us to somehow find Christmas tonight.*

On impulse, I found myself heading toward the little town of Barboursville, West Virginia, a good forty-minute drive. Miss Wilson, I suddenly recalled, had taught art at the junior high school there for thirty-one years. In my work as an editor and photo stylist for home decorating magazines, I'd visited several of her former students' homes.

Once in familiar territory, Miss Wilson began to take in the splendor of Christmas. "This is Jenny Black's home," I said, pointing to the two-story white house on Main Street. "Remember, she used to be Jenny Call. You taught her seventh-grade art."

She rolled down her car window. "Just look at that picket fence draped with evergreens. And there's a candle and wreath in every window. Why, it's a perfect balance of color, texture, and scale," she said, slipping into the artist's vernacular. "Look at that lamp in the window. I can almost smell bread baking. I always told those girls, 'Someday you're going to be homemakers.' Do you suppose she learned any of that from me?"

We drove past Barboursville Junior High, then past homes of other former students whose dazzling doors, lawns, and lampposts showcased the possible influence of a beloved art teacher. Pointing to an old wooden wheelbarrow decked with greenery and a huge red bow, she cried, "Now that's art! Using small things in a great way. Putting the uncommon touch on the common task."

"Speaking of art, do you remember that foggy day when I tried to paint that house way up on the hill?" I quizzed.

"Oh yes," she answered with a chuckle. "You painted it a vibrant red and made it so large that it looked like it was just across the street."

"You always told me, 'Now remember, things look smaller and lighter far away. We call that perspective,' " I lightly teased her. *Perspective*, I thought. That's exactly what I needed now. Something to make my problems look smaller and lighter. We drove on to Stamford Park, where the streets were lined with welcoming luminarias. A giant Christmas card and a life-size manger scene retold the Christmas story in vivid detail. "Candles in paper bags," Miss Wilson gasped. "Well, I've never seen the like. But there's art in everything if you make the best of what you have."

As we drove along we reminisced about the countless art lessons she'd given me over the years. It seemed we'd tried it all—tole painting, stenciling, needlework, papier mâché. And all year long, we'd crafted one-of-a-kind Christmas presents. We'd always had a great time with a little bit of nothing, for Miss Wilson saved everything and stored it all in her wonderful spare bedroom upstairs.

Once, when decorating a dollhouse, I'd grumbled that I had no money for store-bought furnishings. "Why, what you need is all around you," she had answered incredulously. So I studied top-of-the-line catalogs and invented new uses for old objects. Soon I had transformed a braided place mat into an area rug, a crocheted doily into a banquet cloth, and cameo earrings into charming silhouette pictures. Miss Wilson was simply delighted.

I pointed to two homes in the distance. "We just photographed them for next year's Christmas stories," I said. "I can't wait till you see the pictures in the magazine."

"I always knew you'd do something special," she answered. "You were so full of ideas and ingenuity. And never mind that you couldn't draw. You always had that artist's flair."

I could hardly believe three hours had passed. "Need any bread or milk from the grocery store before we head home?" I asked.

"No, but how about running by the corner drugstore to check their after-Christmas markdowns?" she suggested with a newfound sparkle in her voice. "I noticed their sale advertised in today's paper."

"What did you have in mind?" I asked.

"Oh . . ." She paused before continuing. "Just some gift

wrap and cards—you know—for next Christmas. I'll pay you back when we get home. I learned, a long time ago, that to have a blessed Christmas, you need to plan ahead."

Once inside the pharmacy, I grabbed an armload of half-priced wrapping paper for each of us. Suddenly I caught myself humming "Hark the Herald Angels Sing."

"Already in the spirit of Christmas for next year?" the clerk queried.

"Well, I almost missed Christmas this year," I admitted, "but I found it just in time. I want to get an early start on next year."

As I walked back to the car, I reflected on the long-ago first Christmas. What had seemed then like a lowly manger of hay was actually the bed for the King of Kings. It was all in how one looked at things. In three short hours my own eyes had been opened to ever-new possibilities. As Miss Wilson had once told me, "What you need is all around you." My circumstances and problems didn't actually change, of course, just my outlook on them. My hope and joy were back. And to think I almost missed it all!

I'd asked God to help us find Christmas and, hearing my simple prayer, He'd done exactly that. He used a winter outing and an unexpected art lesson to create some much-needed distance between my problems and me.

Ask any artist—things appear smaller and lighter far away. It's all a matter of perspective.

—ROBERTA MESSNER
Kenova, West Virginia

A Christmas Family Reunion

HIRTY-TWO YEARS AGO, I gave up my baby boy for adoption. It was an extremely painful decision, but one I felt was right at the time. I had discovered I was pregnant just shortly after my fiancé, Bob, had broken off our engagement. I was heartbroken, but chose not to tell Bob about the pregnancy because I didn't want him to stay with me just because of the baby. I had three other children from a former marriage I was trying to raise on my own, and I knew how difficult it would be to give love and attention to yet another baby. I felt that adoption was truly in the baby's best interest. In 1965, adoptions were very hush-hush and I had no information about the adoptive couple, but felt certain my baby would be placed with a good, loving family.

It was a very bleak day in December that year when I gave birth to, and then gave away, my son. It is a pain too exquisite to describe. A few days after the birth, Bob, still unaware of his child, called to tell me he had made a big mistake. Stunned, I listened as he explained how the months apart had made him realize his love for my three children and me. He now was certain he wanted to dedicate his life to us. I still refrained from telling him about our son, again not wanting to pressure him into making a commitment to me if he was unsure. In retrospect, I now realize how wrong I was to keep it from him, and that decision would be something for which we would both pay a terrible price.

We were married a month later, and a few weeks after that, I broke the news to him. Completely shocked, Bob announced that we must try to get our baby back, and immediately made arrangements to see the adoption attorney. Nervous and elated at the same time, we drove to his office, excitedly discussing what we would name the baby who would soon be ours again. Even though we knew the other family had been calling the baby by another name for almost two months now, we would rename him: he would be Eric Robert. We offered to reimburse all monies and allow the adoptive family any visitation rights they desired. After we eagerly told the attorney of our decision, he replied, "That is all well and good, but it is not possible, because the baby is no longer alive."

Bob and I clung to each other in disbelief, not able to move or speak. Through tears, Bob finally asked where our little son was buried, but we were told the information was confidential. The attorney then told us the interview was concluded and showed us out.

The years passed and we had another son, but the pain of losing the little boy we never knew left deep scars on our souls. Bob became ill and passed away only eight years later. I remember the morning of his death, after years of silence, quietly talking about our little boy and all the "what ifs." Before Bob closed his eyes for the last time he said, "I guess I'll see him before you do."

I have endured many losses in my life, but I have also been richly blessed through the years. And Christmas 1996 would bring the most unexpected and wonderful gift of all. As I was busily preparing for another holiday season, surrounded by children and grandchildren, I received a phone call from my eighty-five-year-old mother in California. She told me a man had contacted her who claimed to be my son, even though she knew my son had died thirty-one years earlier. She told me the man had some medical concerns about his birth parents, and she urged me to call him. When she told me his name was Eric Robert I thought my heart would burst.

My son, my long-lost son—was it possible? Could I allow myself to believe it? Was this some kind of miracle? Why had I been told he was dead—and why was I receiving this shocking news now, after the pain had been buried so deeply? Why not when his father was still alive? And his name—how was that possible? Bob and I had chosen that name on the way to the attorney's office six weeks after the baby was born, and had told no one. I cried, I shouted, I paced back and forth. Then, with my heart racing, I made the phone call that would begin the healing.

Eric and I spoke for over three hours that first night. He had a son who had died the year before from a genetic condition and he had some questions about his medical background. Our conversation was a bit formal at first, but after I explained how we had tried to get him back and how we had thought he was dead all these years, we cried and laughed together and began to feel a connection. There were so many similarities—we had so much in common although we had never even met. The conversation was not only the beginning of a beautiful new relationship with my son, but also with his wife and their four children. I love being "Nana" to them and we have all had warm and cozy conversations every week since that first night.

Of all the gifts I have ever received, my son's return to my life is supreme. I feel that it was truly a Christmas gift from a loving Father in heaven, just as His Son's birth was a gift to all the world. Perhaps our feet have been guided along similar paths for many years, and those paths will eventually lead us to the same destination. I also hope to someday meet the wonderful parents who raised and nurtured Eric. I am so grateful to them for loving him, and never want to jeopardize his relationship with them.

A few days before Christmas I received a package from Eric's wife—a beautiful picture album of Eric's life from the time he was a baby until the present. As I turned each page and recognized the resemblance to my other children in his face, I felt as if I held my son's life in my hands at long last. Although that album has brought me unspeakable joy, I am eagerly anticipating the day when I can actually hold Eric in my arms and tell him face to face how much I've missed him.

It's often said that the real spirit of Christmas occurs

whenever there are children present. But even though I had children around me, I waited more than thirty years for a Christmas when the one missing child in my life would fill the emptiness in my heart.

—PATRICIA GARRETT
Corvallis, Montana

Patricia was finally able to hold her son, Eric, in her arms the next summer. He has since met the siblings he never knew, and his four children continue to adore their new "Nana."

Against All Odds

M Y WIFE AND I were blessed with four great kids—Jon and his twin brother Paul, Steven, and Sheila. It wasn't long after they were born that all three boys were diagnosed with Duchenne's muscular dystrophy. At that time, even the most optimistic prognosis gave them fifteen to seventeen years to live, most of which time would be spent confined to a wheelchair.

Our sons were more fortunate than most and we were lucky enough to have them with us for twenty-two, twenty-three, and twenty-four years respectively. While most children with this disease never get past elementary school, all three of our boys went to regular schools where they were on the honor roll and all were in college when they passed away. They didn't rely on wheelchairs until about age twelve, and although they eventually wore braces up to their chests and had steel rods implanted the entire length of their spines, they seldom complained. The three of them were a great support to each other—there wasn't anything they couldn't figure out together and they never felt sorry for themselves. Short as their time was on this earth, they made the most of it, enriching the lives of all those with whom they came in contact.

Our Christmas miracle of 1990 involved our oldest son, Jon. In November he was taken to Strong Memorial Hospital in Rochester, New York, 117 miles from our home in Salamanca. He was diagnosed with pneumonia and was treated accordingly. My wife, Ginger, and I went to see him almost every day and his condition seemed to be improving, but on the tenth day he took a turn for the worse. The hospital called us and said they had moved him into intensive care.

When we arrived, we found him on life support, a tracheotomy tube in his throat, and barely able to speak. It was all we could do not to let him see the tears in our eyes. That night we prayed as we never had before. Over the next several days, through written notes he expressed the fact that he had been dependent on an electric wheelchair for so many years, he didn't want to depend on a machine any more to keep him alive. He would write on my hand, "Dad, pull the plug." It wasn't that Jon wanted to die, but to him, a shorter, more normal life without the machine was better than the prospect of months or years on life support in his present condition. Jon's only request was that we please let him go home for Christmas. If he had to die, he wanted to die in the comfort and loving surroundings of his own home, detached from tubes and wires.

His doctor told him it would be impossible for him to go

home since there wouldn't be the professional care or equipment he would need, not to mention the risks posed by the 117-mile ride in an ambulance. "I'm afraid it would take a miracle to do that," the doctor said. But as I looked at Jon's pleading eyes, at the eyes of his two nurses standing at the foot of his bed, and into the tear-filled eyes of his mother, it seemed they were all saying, *Couldn't we at least try?*

We could and we would. After all Jon had been through, and against all odds, our own Christmas Day miracle began to take shape. With the support of a good Dr. Moxley, who had known Jon for many years, we started to get the help we needed. The respiratory therapist taught us how to monitor Jon's breathing, the nurses showed us how to operate and clean the trache, and many other hospital staff members became "angels of mercy," training us how best to care for Jon once we got him home. The doctor in charge, however, was certain Jon would die during the trip home, and refused to take responsibility for what we were about to do. He insisted that we contact the county coroner as well as a funeral director before the day they would release him.

I got in touch with Salamanca's fire chief, Jack McClune, a lifelong friend, who told me he would try to get a crew. The next day he called and said he had three other men who had agreed to make the six- or seven-hour trip on Christmas Day to pick Jon up and bring him home. At 5:00 A.M. on a snowy, blustery New York morning, they picked me up in the city's brand-new ambulance and we made the three-hour drive to the hospital in somewhat difficult conditions.

When we arrived, the nurses had Jon ready and waiting to go. He was still on life support but I saw the first smile on his face I had seen in a long time. After we had said good-bye, thanked all the doctors and nurses, gotten final instructions, and said a silent prayer, Jon was taken off life support. He was on his own. I wished everyone a merry Christmas and the ambulance crew got him ready to travel.

We arrived home about three hours later without any problems. The crew got Jon situated in his bedroom and then were off to be with their own families—for a very late Christmas celebration. These four dedicated men—Jack McClune, Steve Bias, Bill Kendt, and Gene Haugh—had voluntarily sacrificed most of their day, and time with their own families, to bring a dying boy home for Christmas. When I tried to thank them, they simply replied that seeing Jon's smile when he was brought into the house with his family around him was all the thanks they needed. They all agreed that it was the best Christmas they had ever known, and they would have stayed till midnight if Jon had needed the help. When I asked Jack for the ambulance bill, he said that someone in town had heard of our plight and had taken care of it. There would be no charge, and we never did find out who paid for it.

When they left, Ginger and I just stood at the edge of Jon's bed and quietly said a prayer of thanks. Jon was breathing regularly, and best of all, there was a smile on his face I can still see to this day. Later that evening, Jon's brothers, sister, grandparents, aunts, uncles, and cousins joined us for our traditional Christmas turkey dinner. In a chair between his mom and me sat our own Christmas miracle.

Jon was expected to die on Christmas Day, 1990. He lived

to see yet another Christmas and was enrolled in college again when he passed away in March 1992. Jon was never a quitter. He had given all those around him twenty-two years of happiness, spirit, and a love of life we will never forget. And he proved—not one, but two Christmases in a row—that miracles truly exist.

—JIM STEPHENS
Loveland, Colorado

A Star of the Past

CHRISTMAS EVOKES A variety of memories. As a young boy I can remember standing amid the spine-tingling joys of electric trains, bicycles, baseball gloves, and skates. As a young father, I recall seeing the starry eyes of my little children as they beheld the wonders of the day. But somewhere in between, there is one Christmas I will never forget.

Christmas 1945 found me serving in the army of occupation in Frankfurt, Germany. The war had ended about seven months before, but most of the city was rubble. Many of the homes left unscathed were taken over for housing of the U.S. military. Three of us officers lived in a three-story house that could easily have served as home for three families.

Each weekday we would go to our office and return in the evening to find the beds meticulously made and the house spotlessly cleaned by an old German woman who was hired by the U.S. Army to be housekeeper for a number of houses in that area. Only occasionally would we see this frail little lady as she busily engaged in her tasks. Our conversations were limited for she spoke no English and our German was poor, but through sign language and smiles we indicated satisfaction with her work.

Weekly I went to the PX to get my ration of candy bars, soap, and incidentals. Although I sometimes grumbled about the poor selection available, I always purchased all I was allowed and put the excess into my footlocker. As Christmas approached, I thought I should give some little gift to the housekeeper, so from my abundance I filled a large cardboard box with candy bars, soap, and cans of fruit juice. In the system of barter among the Germans, my gift to her was worth many, many dollars, but the cost to me was negligible.

Knowing she would not work on Christmas Day, as I left for the office on December 24 I placed my gift box and a Christmas greeting on the table where they would be seen. All day I felt rather smug as I thought of my generous gift. She would be like an heiress in the poverty of her neighborhood.

As I came home in the darkness of the December evening, I saw the dim glow of the lamp filtering through the window. The house was still. My gift and the recipient were gone, but in the glow of that lamp I saw on the table her Christmas note and her gift to me. I had expected no gift, but there it was—all she could afford, and given in the true spirit of Christmas.

On that dimly lit table, along with her painstakingly written "Merry Christmas," were ten old and dog-eared picture postcards—scenes of Frankfurt. It was obvious these were treasures to her, but there was more to the postcards than just the enchanting pictures. She had placed each card on edge and fastened them together so that every two cards formed a point and all ten together formed the Christmas star.

As I looked at the gift and thought of this woman, I could imagine her in the Frankfurt of years before with its bright shops and cheerful crowds. I could see the stately opera house and public buildings, the parks, the bridges. I could see the gaiety of days before the ravages of war, when Frankfurt, her beloved city, was alive and vibrant.

But now Frankfurt was sad and broken and the little housekeeper was old and frail. What could a poor little old lady give? She could only give from her poverty and from her heart, but I knew she had given one of her most prized possessions—her fondest memories of her beloved, beautiful city.

She had little to give, but it was all she had. Fifty years later, as I occasionally run my fingers over the faded pictures on those postcards tucked away in a box, I am reminded of the true spirit of love and giving at Christmastime. And each year as we stand the cards up on a table to form the Christmas star, just as she had in Germany that night, I realize once again that there was far more goodness in her humble gift to me than in the box of easily gained riches I had so proudly left her. She had taught me that.

But the real miracle working in my heart that long-ago night was the sudden knowledge that her star represented another star which appeared nineteen centuries before, and

that the love born of that star could transcend all the bar-
riers of language, race, and religion the world over. Even in
a country and a world torn apart by war, the influence and
love from that first Christmas made brothers of us all.

—JOHN B. MATHESON, JR.
Salt Lake City, Utah

The Christmas Door Prize

ALREADY REGRETTED MY promise to Mrs. Saunders, the coordinator of the annual Christmas bazaar. "Would you donate the door prize this year, dear? Perhaps one of your famous Christmas theme trees," she'd persuaded with a sparkle in her eyes. "We're hoping to make lots of money to play Santa Claus for needy families. And you know, there's nothing like a wonderful door prize to draw shoppers to a bazaar!"

Three months earlier, Mrs. Saunders' simple request hadn't seemed like such a chore. Now, with only three weeks left before the bazaar, the uncompleted task hung over my head like a frost-brittled limb.

It really wasn't like me to put things off until the last minute, but I'd been waiting for a spurt of inspiration. I wanted to craft something really special, something with meaning, not just another decorative accent to end up in someone's summer rummage sale.

So, on the eve of bazaar, I sat at my kitchen table with that sinking feeling in my stomach, staring blankly at a four-foot-tall artificial evergreen, three cartons of twinkling lights, a shoe box full of shimmering ornaments, a bolt of ribbon, and my faithful glue gun. Still, inspiration eluded me.

The next thing I knew, I was crawling in our stuffy attic, poking desperately through boxes and praying for a quick dose of creative genius. I grabbed two boxes of would-be treasures and trudged back to the kitchen. Perhaps some holiday music would put me in a festive mood, I decided, as I popped in a Christmas cassette.

Before long, I was singing the familiar words, "Joy to the world, the Lord is come; let Earth receive her King," as I rummaged through a box labeled OLD DOLLS—DO NOT THROW AWAY. I gazed down at the pile of colorful little dolls I'd purchased at a roadside flea market some years back while on vacation. What had possessed me to buy this motley crew of dolls? After they had been packed away and totally forgotten, their bright costumes now lay in hopeless disarray. I picked up a Japanese doll clothed in a royal blue kimono, a Native American family complete with a brown felt tepee, a "Miss Liberty" doll bedecked in red, white, and blue, and a quartet of dolls dressed in Scandinavian attire.

Suddenly something deep within me shouted the solution: make a "Joy to the World" tree! One by one, I excitedly wired the dolls to the evergreen branches until they nearly sagged from the weight of two dozen dolls. A few of the dolls were in pieces. Painstakingly, I restrung their arms and legs with a pair of tweezers and some rubber bands. As I cupped the dolls in my hands to restring their limbs, I suddenly felt a kinship with women of all nationalities. What I was doing made me realize that there were women the world over who, just like me, needed the love of the Savior of Christmas to put them back together.

Just then my friend Betsy walked through the door to check on my progress. Before we knew it, we were both in full swing decorating the tree. "How about using some of these dried flowers?" Betsy suggested, pointing to bouquets of burgundy cockscombs, delicate baby's breath, and pink sweetheart roses hanging from the kitchen ceiling beams. Next we added snippets of ribbon and lace and hung old-fashioned jeweled ornaments from every branch.

"What are you going to do about that bare spot in the middle?" Betsy asked. "We're all out of dolls." We combed the house until we found the crowning touch: a small world globe from my desk, topped with a velvet bow retrieved from the wreath hanging on my mantel.

We stood back and smiled at our handiwork. "That's the prettiest tree I've ever seen," Betsy concluded. I had to agree with her, but I had the strong feeling that we hadn't completely decorated that tree by ourselves.

The next morning, I carefully packed the "Joy to the World" tree in my car. On impulse, I dashed back into the house and grabbed an extension cord, a portable tape player, and the cassette tape of "Joy to the World."

When I arrived at the bazaar, everyone was in the holiday spirit. A craftswoman strolled over from her booth of patchwork stockings and gently fingered the dolls of all lands. "I'm going to order one of these trees for my granddaughter in Germany," she announced.

Then the gingerbread cookie lady joined in the conversation. "I'm buying three tickets to the bazaar," she joked. "*I'm* going home with this tree."

"This tree will steal the show," Mrs. Saunders piped up. "When word gets out about *our* door prize, there's no telling how much money we'll make. We're sure to surpass our record attendance of a thousand." Before long, the room was packed with a steady stream of shoppers. And all day long, the one-of-a-kind tree was the target of wishful glances.

A few minutes before the scheduled drawing, a tiny woman with tired eyes, wearing a dingy gray coat, exchanged fifty cents for a ticket. Her neatly braided hair coiled tightly into an old-fashioned bun framed a face stripped of everything but determination.

"We came into town to buy feed for the livestock and I talked my husband into stopping here," she said. "Had a little egg money left to spend but he tried to convince me I wouldn't be able to afford much in a fancy place like this."

The woman admired the satin angels, homemade jellies, and a fruitcake baked to resemble a holiday wreath. Her gnarled hands picked up a crocheted snowflake as intricate as a cobweb. "Just look at that," she said. "Someday I'm gonna have me a Christmas tree and load it plumb full of these."

As she approached my booth, she exclaimed, "That tree . . . them dolls! All my life I've wanted a pretty doll. Is someone gonna win *all* them dolls?" she asked with a dreamy look in her eyes.

I flipped on the cassette player and the melody of "Joy to the World" filled the room. "Why, the choir sings that song down to the church," she said. "Always reminds me of them people overseas the missionary lady told us about."

All eyes were now on the person who would soon draw the winning number for the door prize. From all over, I heard whispers: "Don't forget, that tree is *mine* . . . No, it's *mine* . . . It's for my grandchildren who are coming for Christmas . . ."

But the tiny woman never took her eyes off the tree. "My grandson Jake, he lives up the holler from our place," she told me. "He's real smart in book learnin'. Why, he could recite every one of them countries on that globe."

Then came the long-awaited announcement: "The door prize goes to number 1153!" I glanced down at the gnarled hands that held the winning ticket and squeezed her thin shoulders.

"You won the tree! You won the tree!" I cried.

"You mean it's *my* ticket? I ain't never had nothin' nice as this." Tears rolled down her wrinkled cheeks.

I unplugged the lights and tape player and wound the extension cord. "Am I gonna get that music box and long cord, too?" she asked. "I'm settin' that tree in the winder and we only have one outlet in the room. I shore could use that extra cord."

"Of course . . . it's Christmas," I answered as I carried the tree outside for her. A rusted yellow pickup truck pulled up in front and a man wearing bibbed overalls, a plaid flannel shirt, and a cap declaring "I ♥ Kentucky," jumped out. "Sadie, what you got there?" he hollered with a gap-toothed grin.

"Pa, I won a prize! I *won* this tree!"

Quickly, he rearranged a shovel, tire chains, and sacks of

feed to make room for the tree in the bed of the truck. He grabbed his pocket knife and split two empty feed sacks to cover the tree, and secured them with bailing twine. "Can you believe it?" an onlooker gasped. "They're taking that beautiful tree away in that old beat-up truck. What in the world do people like that even need with such a tree?"

I waved good-bye as the clunker truck disappeared into the violet evening sky. In my mind's eye, I could see the tree given a place of honor in the window of a humble, dimly lit cabin in the heart of the Appalachian mountains. The folks who lived there were a happy sort, I told myself. Not world travelers, but hard workers. Black smoke would likely billow from their chimney into the nippy December air as the family gathered around the tree. "Look, Granny, here's Japan," Jake might say, pointing to the globe that once sat on my desk. And Sadie, still fascinated with that extension cord, would plug in the twinkling lights and her "music box."

Yet I'm convinced that I'm the real winner in this American tradition called Christmas bazaars, for discovering anew the calling of believers everywhere. I never saw Sadie again, but I would never forget the lesson she taught me: that regardless of the diversity in our geography or social status, we are all God's extension cords, taking His light and song to the dark and empty places of our world.

—NANCY ANDERSON
Wurtland, Kentucky

The First American Christmas

HE CHRISTMAS LIGHTS made the wet streets of Los Angeles glow with color, but they couldn't lift our gloomy mood. Cold and tired, my wife and I went from store to store in the light drizzle, looking for an inexpensive watch for our nine-year-old son. It was the night before Christmas in 1955, just a few short months after we emigrated to this country. We barely had enough money for food, but Billy talked about nothing but a watch for Christmas. We soon realized that the extra ten dollars we had set aside for his present would not be enough.

Passing a dimly lit jewelry store on our way back to the bus stop, we decided to give it one more try. The elderly proprietor eagerly showed us his wares, but even his cut-rate prices were too high for us. Moving the shiny merchandise back and forth on the counter, the owner noticed my foreign-made watch. He perked up when I told him I'd bought it in Austria.

"Hey, Joey," he called toward the rear of the store, "you ever seen a Zenith self-winder watch overseas?"

From behind the threadbare curtain appeared a young man in his late twenties. He held a broken watch in one hand while with the other he pushed the watchmaker's magnifying glass he wore on his forehead up out of the way. Without even looking up at me, he bent over the counter and focused on my watch.

"Do you still like to read Zane Grey?" my wife asked him quietly.

Joe's head snapped up. His eyes widened with recognition.

"My God, Pia, Gus! What are you doing here? When did you guys come over?" The words came tumbling out of his mouth; he could not believe what he saw.

We had met Joe in Austria, where he served in the occupying armed forces after the Second World War. My wife, Pia, and I worked on the army base as civilian employees. She was a librarian and I ran a hobby shop in the special services club. Joe loved to read Westerns by Zane Grey, and whenever a new edition arrived, Pia put it aside for him. We became good friends and when Joe was shipped back stateside we thought that we would never see each other again. Not in our wildest dreams did Pia and I think that someday we would have a chance to move to America. Yet only seven years later we had arrived, flat broke.

"So, what are you doing now? How do you like it here?" His questions came one after the other. Over the next half hour we told him all about our sponsor, our high hopes for our new life in California, and the reality of the long hours and disappointing low wages that I had found in Los Angeles.

"This is our first trip downtown, and if I'd known the prices, we could have saved the bus fare," I concluded our story. We were ready to leave, but Joe insisted that we pick out a watch and that he would make us a deal. Just to go along with him, we chose a small one with a golden face and a silvery metal band. With a glance at the price tag and an indiscernible nod from his father, Joe announced that while we were making up our minds he would go in the back to look for a suitable box. He retreated behind the curtain again but kept up the conversation, as if to bridge the awkward silence that took the place of our previous lively discussion.

"Here you go—give my best to Billy." Joe emerged from the rear room and handed us a little gift-wrapped box. We started to object but he said, "This is your first Christmas in the States, and my dad and I want you to have a merry one. You have no idea what your friendship meant to me when I was overseas."

Trying to hold back the tears, we thanked him for his generosity and quietly left the store. Outside the bell from the Salvation Army sounded a bit more urgent than before and as my wife and I walked past I reached down and slipped my ten-dollar bill into the red bucket.

On Christmas morning Billy woke us before daylight to show us the watch he had found under the tree. He mumbled excitedly about the Three Kings carrying gold, myrrh, and frankincense to Bethlehem, and for a fleeting moment before I drifted back to sleep again, I thought I could see one of them holding a small gold and silvery object in his hands.

—AUGUST KUND
Camarillo, California

The Secret of Grandma's Sugar Crock

HROUGH THE YEARS, I've discovered bits and pieces of the past that, when put together, make up my extraordinary grandmother Maria Carmela Curci-Dinapoli. I knew that she came to this country as a young immigrant from Italy, and married my grandfather, Antonio Curci, in 1910. A few years later, she was widowed with three children. I had heard family stories of how Grandma struggled to find work, pay her debts, and keep her family together during those difficult years. In all of these stories, one fact remained prominent—Grandma's deep religious devotion had guided her through each problem and task.

But it was only recently that I would discover yet another missing piece to Grandma's past that would help me know her just that much better. My memories of Grandma begin on an Almaden ranch in California during World War II. By then, she had married her second husband, Tony Dinapoli, and had settled into her rural ranch life, raising a family of seven boys and one girl.

During World War II, a government-issued flag, imprinted with five blue stars, hung in the front window of my grandparents' old farmhouse. It meant that five of their sons were off fighting in the war. Without the boys to work the land, the ranch was shorthanded. Grandma and Grandpa had to work twice as hard now to produce a bountiful fruit crop. During harvesttime, every member of the family pitched in to help, including grandkids like myself. Even so, it was a difficult time for Grandma: Rationing was in effect, there was little money, and worst of all there was the constant worry over whether her five sons would come home safely.

The ranch was a lovely place, especially in the spring, when the orchards were white with plum blossoms. During the summer, while we harvested the prune crop, Grandma cooked up fine Italian lunches. We would all sit on blankets spread out over the orchard ground, enjoying not just the wonderful food but also the satisfaction of being a part of such an important family effort.

To encourage the ripe fruit to fall, Grandpa used a long wooden pole with an iron hook at the top to shake the branches of every tree, causing a shower of plums to cover the ground. Then the rest of us would crawl along, wearing kneepads that Grandma had sewn into our overalls, and gather the plums into metal buckets. We dumped the buckets of plums into long wooden trays, where the purple little plums were soon sun-dried into rich, brown prunes.

After a long, hard day I would walk hand in hand with Grandpa through the orchard while he surveyed what had been accomplished that day. I'd enjoy eating fresh plums off the trees, then licking the sweet stickiness from my finger-tips.

On each of these walks, Grandpa would stoop down and pick up a handful of soil, letting it sift slowly and lovingly through his strong, work-callused fingers. Then with pride and conviction he would inevitably say, "If you take good care of the land, the land will take good care of you."

As darkness came, we'd all sit together on the cool, quiet veranda of the front porch. Grandpa would settle comfortably into his rocker, under the dim glow of a flickering moth-covered light bulb, and there he'd read the latest war news in his newspaper. Grandma sat nearby on the porch swing, swaying and saying her perpetual rosary. The stillness of the quiet ranch house painfully reflected the absence of the five robust young men. This was the hardest part of the day for Grandma; the silence of the empty house was a painful reminder that her sons were far, far away fighting for their country.

On Sunday morning, after church, Grandma was back out on the porch, again repeating her rosary before going into the kitchen to start cooking. Then she and Grandpa sat at the kitchen table, counting out ration slips for the week ahead and what little cash there was to pay the bills. Once they were finished, Grandma always took a portion of her money and put it in the sugar crock, placing it high on the kitchen shelf. I often asked her what the money in the jar was for. She would simply answer, "A very special favor."

Well, the war finally ended, and all five of Grandma's sons

came home remarkably safe and sound. After a while, Grandma and Grandpa retired, and their little farm became part of a modern expressway.

I never did find out what the money in the sugar crock was for—until a week or so before last Christmas. Completely on impulse, perhaps feeling the wonder of the Christmas season and the need to connect with its spiritual significance, I stopped at a little church I just happened to be driving past. I'd never been inside before, and as I entered the church through the side door, I was stunned to come face to face with the most glorious stained-glass window.

I stopped to examine the intricate beauty of the window more closely. The magnificent stained glass depicted the Holy Mother and Child, and like an exquisite jewel, it reflected the glory of the very first Christmas. As I studied every detail of its fine workmanship, I found, to my utter amazement, a small plaque that read, "For a favor received— donated in 1945 by Maria Carmela Curci-Dinapoli." I couldn't believe it—I was reading my grandmother's very words! Every day, as Grandma had said her prayers for her soldier sons, she'd also put whatever money she could scrape together into her sacred sugar crock to pay for the window. Her quiet donation of this window had been her way of saying thank you to God for sparing the lives of her beloved five sons.

The original church in which the window was placed had long ago been torn down. Through the generations, the family had lost track of its existence.

Finding this window at Christmas, more than half a century later, not only brought back a flood of memories from those World War II days on the ranch, but also made me a believer in small but beautiful miracles.

—COOKIE CURCI-WRIGHT
San Jose, California

The Christmas Tea

O BE A person to whom a miracle has happened is to be a person transformed. Such was the case for me in December of 1993.

After not attending church much since my childhood, I had taken it up again. This time it was because I wanted to go to church, though, not because someone dragged me there. In order to become more involved in my new church, Crossroads Baptist Church, I joined the women's ministries program. And in order to become more involved in women's ministries, I volunteered to help at the annual Christmas tea.

My task seemed manageable enough. I'd been charged with preparing the food for the tea—220 small tea sandwiches and 220 small pastries. I was excited. Not only had I not been much of a churchgoer, but I also hadn't been much of a volunteer in life. This was my chance to take the plunge and really help out in a big way. And I planned to do it right.

The week before the tea, I decided that for the sweet, I would make 220 small angel food cake rolls. I'd seen the recipe in one of my recipe books, but who has the occasion to make something as fancy as that in everyday life? Now I had the occasion. The little cakes looked so beautiful in the photograph, and the directions seemed easy enough. It went something like this: Take an angel food loaf cake and cut it lengthwise into four strips. Spread the strips with jam. Roll each strip and then cut in half for a miniature jelly roll. Each loaf cake would make 8 jelly rolls. So for 220 women I would need . . . 30 angel food loaf cakes. I tried the recipe using an angel food loaf cake that I bought at the grocery store. It didn't seem too bad.

I ordered thirty angel food loaf cakes from a local bakery. My plan was to make the cakes on Thursday and Friday, in plenty of time for our tea on Saturday afternoon. I arrived at the bakery Thursday morning to pick up my angel food cakes. Once home, I rolled up my sleeves and started to work. This was going to be great!

No, this was not going to be great at all—the angel food cakes were raw in the middle! Trying not to panic, I raced back to the bakery. They were quite apologetic and told me that they had twenty cakes in the freezer. The remaining cakes would be baked and ready the next day. Relieved, I drove home with my twenty angel food cakes.

Then the nightmare began in earnest. These cakes were not like the one I had practiced on. The knife stuck. The cakes tore. The result was a disaster. At 2:00 A.M. I had finished making 160 pathetic-looking jelly rolls. I wanted to cry. I had hoped for—in fact I had promised—a culinary triumph that would be the talk of the Christmas tea. And look what I had—160 crumbling, jagged, malformed jelly rolls.

Friday morning I was determined to start fresh, with new angel food cakes. I called the local bakery and told them not to make my remaining ten cakes. I started driving to every bakery in town. Many of the bakeries had angel food tube cakes, but loaf cakes were scarce. Every one told me that they could custom-bake the loaf cakes for me, but I no longer had time for that. The tea was the very next day. I was panic-stricken. I had only one bakery outlet left. This was my last chance.

As I've mentioned, I was pretty new to churchgoing. And pretty new to the idea of prayer. I thought people just prayed for big things, and that you wouldn't bother God with the minor details of life. But as I drove toward that last bakery outlet with tears streaming down my face, I began to pray: "Dear God, please may there be angel food loaf cakes here. Not the tube kind, the loaf kind, God. Please, God. This Christmas tea is for you." I parked my car and walked into the bakery. Directly in front of me as I walked through the sliding glass doors were rows of angel food loaf cakes. I became so excited, the cashier must have thought a crazy woman had just walked through her door. These were the lightest, fluffiest, best-looking angel food cakes I'd ever seen. Holding my breath, I began to count. There were seventeen cakes on the rack. My heart skipped. "Do you have any more cakes in the back?" I asked the cashier.

"We don't normally carry this kind," she replied. "They arrived just a few minutes ago and I only had time to put these out. Sure, we have more in the back. I'll get them for you." I loaded my car with angel food cakes. And on my way home, instead of crying tears of frustration, I cried tears of joy.

As I set up my worktable in the kitchen once again, I knew it would be close. I hadn't bothered to count, but I knew that I didn't have any extra cakes for mishaps. I figured that if I was short, I would bring along some of the ugly cakes I'd made and serve those to my table. My knife slid through these new cakes like butter. The little jelly rolls I made this time were as pretty as the picture in the cookbook. I worked all afternoon and evening with my knife and pots of jam, finishing the last of the cakes at ten o'clock Friday night. Tired but satisfied, I began to count my little beauties. Do you know how many cakes I had? Exactly 220 . . . 220 beautiful angel food jelly rolls. Not one too many. Not one shy.

Four years later I am still awestruck by this story. It still brings tears to my eyes when I think of my first Christmas tea. God sent me those angel food cakes from heaven. Just as surely as God is involved in any miracle, I know He was involved in mine. I am not the same person I was back then; my life is filled with a sense of peace that only a faith in God can bring. God's love is all around us; it can be found in the tiniest of details. Merry Christmas—and do come to our Christmas tea if you're ever in my town. Now I'm the director of it!

—LYNNE HALL
Mukilteo, Washington

One Tiny Miracle

A S A TECHNICIAN trained on the job with less than six months' experience, I felt a little naked in the hospital's neonatal intensive-care unit in Kirksville, Missouri. It was December 1980. My hands were big; the babies were so small that it often seemed impossible to work with them without harming them. Even so, the unit was my favorite part of the hospital. Life began there. Every day before I left at 7:00 A.M., I would see new mothers and fathers proudly pushing their babies about the halls. I grieved for the parents whose newborns still lay in the intensive-care unit, their future uncertain.

I arrived one night to find that the head of the unit at the time, Wynn Douglas, was working nights with us. I peered over his shoulder at the tiniest infant I had ever seen.

"Tony," he said, "meet Brian." It almost seemed that, from beneath the lifelines linking his body to the ventilator, a frail little hand waved at me. But I knew better. When I held Brian in my hand, his tiny legs barely reached my wrist. After his premature birth, his weight dropped to three pounds. He looked smaller. His eyes, which were closed tightly against the overhead lights that gave him warmth, were like tiny slits. His color was ashen.

"He's awfully small, Wynn!" I said.

"He's awfully strong," Wynn replied. There was something in his voice that made me take notice. This wasn't a professional statement; this was a personal observation. This was the kind of statement others had counseled against: "Don't become involved with your patients."

"You staying the night?" I asked. "Yeah," he said rubbing his eyes, looking at his watch. "Relieve me at two o'clock, will you?" At first I didn't know what to say. I didn't have a lot of experience with ventilators, and certainly not with neonatal ventilators. "What if I come at one o'clock and you teach me what I need to know?"

Wynn agreed and off I went to take care of routine patients on the medical floors below. When I reflect on that chance encounter now, I think it probably changed my life. At 1:00 A.M., I dutifully returned and Wynn began the long process of instructing me on the ventilator. The nurse cast a fretful eye toward us as Wynn explained the machine— what it did and why we used it.

"The main thing to look out for," he told me, "is that the endotracheal tube into the lungs doesn't get kinked, plugged, or, worse yet, pulled out." He reviewed emergency procedures and told me to page him if anything went wrong while he ate his lunch. With my stomach in knots, I agreed to call him and silently said a prayer that nothing would go wrong, at least for the thirty minutes that I had the watch. Those thirty minutes seemed like a full shift. Every twitch of Brian's tiny body sent me into an overreactive spasm. Every change in the sound of his heart monitor sent adrenaline surging through my veins. I was very glad to see Wynn when he strolled back through the doors of the unit. Yet, like a junkie who survives his first high, I found that that first shift resulted in a need to be involved in Brian's care. I started going back to the unit whenever I found Wynn there—and that was frequently those first few weeks in December.

He taught me how to use the transcutaneous monitor (to determine how much oxygen was in the blood), how to suction mucus from Brian's airways, and how to be as much help to the nurses as possible. As I learned about infants, I began to understand Wynn's personal observation about Brian's strength. Brian was indeed a fighter. Though tiny and afflicted with respiratory distress caused by his immature lungs, he overcame every obstacle in his way. During those first two weeks, he was making great strides. His color improved, and he gained weight. It seemed that Brian would defy the odds against such a small infant surviving. Brian had been born in a tiny hospital in northern Missouri, between twenty-four and twenty-six weeks' gestation. A team had been dispatched from our hospital, Kirksville College of Osteopathic Medicine Hospital, to pick Brian up and bring him to our neonatal intensive-care unit. Under the care of our neonatologist and a team of nurses and therapists, he made much better progress than anyone expected. The week before Christmas that year, we had planned to remove his breathing tube. I'm still not clear on what had caused his setback. Brian was now in critical condition. The constant rush of air pumped into his lungs by the ventilator had damaged them. We adjusted the percentage of oxygen delivered by the life-support equipment on an almost endless basis, trying to keep his oxygen at adequate levels.

On December 23, I went in to pick up my paycheck and found Wynn looking glum. He explained that he was going to ruin someone's Christmas. Someone was going to have to stay at Brian's bedside around the clock. Special-duty respiratory care would be required because the holiday schedules left us with even fewer therapists. But Wynn wasn't worried about asking someone to work on Christmas; someone had to do that anyway. He was worried that whoever was on duty might have to take part in an unsuccessful attempt to resuscitate Brian.

I had no family and no plans for Christmas. I told him I would consider it an honor to work over the holidays. At first, he was dubious. I was the most interested but least qualified therapist he had, but when no one else volunteered, he reluctantly agreed. We settled on doing twelve-hour shifts each.

Christmas Eve night was very difficult. While all the world was thinking about peace on earth, here I was holding the hand of an infant who might never know the joy of seeing colored lights on a tree. With every fluctuation of blood pressure, with every minor crisis, I saw tears well up in the eyes of the nurse assigned to care for Brian. I don't know how many prayers I said that night, but I know they were many. It was a long night. Countless cups of coffee were consumed. We made about a hundred adjustments to the ventilator. The ventilator flow sheet, where patient data was recorded, was about the length of a novel. At about 3:00 A.M. that night, Brian somehow disconnected himself from the breathing tube, and we had to hand-ventilate him for twenty minutes until the neonatologist arrived to reinsert the tube.

The doctor, a kind and gentle man, never questioned our technique or asked us, "How could this happen?" He just reinserted the tube and took up a lonely vigil with the rest of us. He stayed with us until it was time for him to go home and open presents with his children.

When I left the unit that morning, I thought it would be my last shift taking care of Brian. I slept fitfully, dreaming about an infant I seemed powerless to make better. I went to work early on Christmas Day and ran into the neonatologist searching for blood donors. "What type do you need?" I asked. "O positive!" he said. A type and crossmatch later, I sat pumping my arm, feeding a collection bag full of my O positive blood for Brian. Between Christmas and New Year's Day, I spent each night pulling a twelve-hour shift in the nursery. Every day held a crisis or two, and every time Brian would bounce back and keep fighting.

The nursery staff seemed almost transformed by Brian. His spunk and drive inspired everyone. That is how I will remember that Christmas. I received the best gift any health-care worker can ever receive: the bonding that occurs when a patient survives in some small part because of the effort you make. For Brian got better. Four months after he came to our hospital, he left. He left whole, neurologically intact, and without "retrolental fibroplasia," a prevalent eye disorder in neonates caused by high oxygen concentrations during life support. Brian's neonatologist attributed the prevention of this disorder to the one-on-one care Brian received from a select group of therapists.

The nursing staff made a quilt for Brian. We took turns instructing the family on CPR, oxygen therapy, and other supportive measures he might need at home. By the time he left, Brian had shown us all a thing or two about courage and love, and about ourselves too. And I received yet another gift: I met my future wife during those long, lonely vigils in the unit.

Brian is eleven years old today, and I understand he is living a normal life in northern Missouri. I hope he reads this. I've always wanted to tell him thanks—thanks for everything. And thanks for teaching a handful of adults a thing or two about courage and love.

—A. L. DeWitt
St. Louis, Missouri

Abbey's Lucky Day

EN INCHES OF fresh powder had fallen overnight, and the sun shone down on one of those glorious Tahoe days. After a picture-perfect white Christmas in the Sierras, the first week of January was just breathtaking.

I had other things to do this day, one of which was to mail a letter attempting to bring closure to a two-year relationship. And as bright as the sun shone, things were still a bit gray.

So, in an attempt to break my mental logjam, I grabbed my telemark skis, packed a lunch, and headed out to climb Mount Tallac. Telemark skiing is like a cross between downhill and cross-country: you walk up and ski down. You wear skins on the bottom of your skis to help with traction on the climb up.

Now for the seasoned telemark skier, Tallac was a mere two-hour jaunt there and back. My last attempt, however, had been a four-hour death ski, leaving me crawling up the last steps to the peak.

This time, I made my way to the base and began to climb without hesitation. I pushed my skis uphill through three feet of fresh powder until the track climbed vertically before me. I was in a descending track, making it nearly impossible to climb. I made a few attempts, but my climbing skins wouldn't stick, and twice I fell backward into hip-deep powder. I poled, pushed, pulled, and squirmed, then swore— loudly. I was stuck like a fly in a jar of Vaseline.

After finally freeing myself, I decided to traverse the mountainside in search of an ascending track. As I trudged through the impossible powder, it seemed as though nothing in my life of late was working out. Just then, one of my skins peeled off. I stepped off my ski, and my leg sank into the snow up to my hip. I nearly gave up, but instead pointed my skis toward the sun and gently pushed forward for nearly an hour, ascending halfway up the mountain.

Shortly thereafter, I spied a beautiful sight. It was a set of ascending tracks. I was saved. I traversed up the tracks with ease, stopping momentarily to gaze at the cobalt-blue water of Lake Tahoe below me, juxtaposed with the jagged white peaks above.

The scenery seemed to energize me, driving me upward. I came upon a small overlook nearly 1,500 feet up when something out of place caught my eye.

It was a dog, small and brown with large pointy ears and dark, sullen eyes. I called out and waited for its master to come around the corner to greet me. Then I looked around and yelled out again. Nothing. I scanned the freshly fallen snow. There were no footprints, nor were there incoming or outgoing ski tracks. I realized I was the only skier on the mountain.

I pulled off my skis and made my way down the steep ascent to where the dog had built a platform in the snow. Again I called out. Nothing. I inspected the impromptu nest and it seemed to tell a desperate story. There was frozen blood, urine, and various droppings. I approached the dog slowly and checked the collar. Her tags were from San Mateo, California, her name was Abbey, and she was many miles from home. She was hypothermic, critically weak, and cold. She couldn't walk and shivered as I held her frostbitten and bloodied feet. The puncture wounds reminded me that the coyotes I had seen on my last ascent were probably still around.

This was Abbey's lucky day.

I encouraged Abbey to walk, but she couldn't. Without hesitation, I wrote off reaching the summit. I determined that I'd have to carry Abbey down the hill. For a strong telemark skier, this may have been pretty straightforward. But for me, it was a formidable task. I tried diligently to fit her into my day pack, but she was too big. I reassured her, then strapped her to the outside of my pack. Her packaging was an exercise in futility, as her butt hung out one side and her head the other. I thought to myself how difficult downhill telemark skiing was without a sixty-pound dog strapped to your back, and likened the task to skating on marbles while carrying a half-empty barrel of water.

Amazingly, I fell only twice, descending slowly until my legs were burning with pain. Each time I got up, she looked at me as if to show her appreciation. When I finally got to my truck, my shoulders were raw. I gave her a bit of my Power Bar, thinking she might be too weak to eat, but she ate it without hesitation. I knew she'd been up there for more than one night.

When I entered the Alpine Animal Hospital with Abbey in my arms, the receptionist looked up the numbers on her tag and found out that she happened to be one of the hospital's patients. In addition, there was a desperately scrawled note on the wall, searching for a dog named Abbey.

Shortly thereafter, I was on the phone with her owner, who was nearly in tears. It turned out that that Abbey had been missing for more than nine days. She'd wandered off during Christmas festivities at a local cabin. The veterinarian looked her over, caring for her various injuries. Just as I headed for the door, Abbey looked up as if to say, "Thank you." In that moment, I realized heartaches were only temporary.

—RICK GUNN
South Lake Tahoe, California

On Wings of Faith

ACH YEAR AT Christmas children lie awake at night hoping to hear the sound of reindeer hooves prancing lightly on the rooftop. But children are not easily fooled, and as they grow older they ask adults many intelligent questions: Is it really possible that Santa Claus can fly through the air in a sleigh without engine or wings? But if a child asked me, I would have to say, "Yes!" Yes, it is possible for a man to fly through the air without help. Because it happened to me last December.

It was a very cold and wintry Saturday. I am a doctor, the sort of doctor who takes care of all kinds of patients, from delivering babies to helping families say their last farewells to the elderly. In addition to my practice in Hoisington, Kansas, I am also a member of the Board of Healing Arts, the state medical licensing board. Our meetings are held every other month in Topeka. And so it was on that early Saturday morning that I left home for the monthly meeting.

Now this is a trip that can take hours by car, so instead of driving, I fly fifty minutes in my plane, a Comanche 400. I've been flying for years and am very comfortable in the cockpit. And that Saturday seemed no different.

I checked the weather conditions at the airport before going out to my plane. It was 20 degrees, with a windchill of zero. Cold, but not dangerous. I'd certainly flown in those conditions before. In fact, I'd made the trip to Topeka so many times that much of the trip I relied on autopilot. I'd set the instruments up for a direct flight to Topeka and not take them off autopilot until I was ready to land. It gave me time to clear my mind of the week's work problems and get in the proper frame of mind for the business of the licensing board.

Despite the cold, the sky was clear. I left Great Bend airport at 7:15 A.M., taking off just as the sun was rising. To heat up the cockpit, I turned on both the defrost and the heater. I climbed to 5,500 feet and began to adjust my instruments for a direct flight to Topeka. I adjusted my GPS (global positioning satellite), set my radio to the frequencies of the airports I would be passing, chose the proper settings for my other gauges, and turned on the autopilot. Then I relaxed to enjoy the flight.

About thirty minutes into the flight, I remember flying over the small town of Herington. That was always my signal to set my instruments up for a Topeka landing. I adjusted my radio to the Topeka airport tower, listened to the weather reports, and turned on my NDB (nondirectional beacon). It was about 7:45 A.M., and I had about five to ten minutes before my actual landing in Topeka. What happened next has renewed my faith in miracles.

Suddenly I woke up. I didn't know I had been asleep, but all at once I was awake. It was 9:30 A.M. I was disoriented and thought I was still in the air. Frantically, I began to adjust the throttle and put down the landing gear. I thought I was on the approach to Topeka and had somehow dozed off for a few seconds. But try as I might, my instruments were not responding to my efforts. I was about to crash! I looked up from my instrument panel to see a strange sight— in front of me was a line of trees, level with my plane. I looked out the side window to see an even stranger sight— my plane was sitting on the ground. I had already crashed!

I sat in the cockpit for a few minutes, trying to clear my head. Slowly I climbed out of the plane and stood next to it. The landscape didn't look at all familiar. Where was I? There was a farmhouse in the distance, so I set off toward it.

The farmer who answered the door was suspicious of my tale. A plane had crashed in his field? He hadn't heard a thing. But by craning his neck in the direction I pointed, he could see my crippled plane resting in his field, each wing caught on a tree. He quickly called for help.

As it turned out, I wasn't in Kansas anymore. While we waited for help to arrive, the farmer told me I was in Cairo, Missouri, straight north of Columbia by about thirty miles. Dumbfounded, I asked for a map. Tracing the route with my finger, I realized that my plane had flown directly over Topeka on autopilot and as far as the fuel in my tank could take me. The plane then left the sky and glided gracefully into a hayfield.

But how? And why? Why had I not been awake? The answers came later at the hospital. A toxic screen of my blood revealed extremely high levels of carbon monoxide. Further investigation of my wrecked plane showed that there was a crack in the right muffler. In airplanes, the muffler is tied into the heating system, so by turning on the heat that cold morning I had been filling the cockpit with carbon monoxide.

I am incredibly lucky to be alive. I passed out thousands of feet above the ground; and I truly do feel that God took the controls from there and brought me down safely. All I came away with was a small cut, a broken wrist, and a severe headache from the fumes.

So yes, if a small child asks me at Christmas if Santa can fly, I will just smile wisely. Because sometimes, when you go up in the air, faith takes over.

—DR. BOB FRAYSER
Hoisington, Kansas

Would you like to share your miracle?
We would love to hear about the
miracles in your life, whether
they happened at Christmas
or any other time of year.
Please send your story to:

❉

JENNIFER BASYE SANDER

"MIRACLES"

P.O. BOX 2463

GRANITE BAY, CA

95746-2463

❉

Please include your address and phone
number so we can contact you.

$\mathcal{A}\,\mathcal{C}\,\mathcal{K}\,\mathcal{N}\,\mathcal{O}\,\mathcal{W}\,\mathcal{L}\,\mathcal{E}\,\mathcal{D}\,\mathcal{G}\,\mathcal{M}\,\mathcal{E}\,\mathcal{N}\,\mathcal{T}\,\mathcal{S}$

Our warmest thanks and deepest gratitude to the talented people at William Morrow, especially our fabulous editor, Toni Sciarra, and associate editor Katharine Cluverius. We are also indebted to our wonderful agent, Sheree Bykofsky.

This book would not have been possible without the contributions of the following; we thank them so much for their time, effort, and support: Bill Adler, Jr.; Xan Albright; Keith Anderson; Edward Andrusko; Kerstin Backman; the Basye family; Dian Bradshaw; Amy Bryan; Candy Chand; Sue Martin Cook; Delys Waite Cowles; Cookie Curci-Wright; Chuck and Barbara Curtis; Paul DeBor; A. L. DeWitt; Gloria S. Dittman; James Dodson; Gwen Ellis; Bettina Flores; Terry Foley; Bob Frayser; Hope Gardner; Patricia Garrett; the Glassover family; Rick Gunn; Lynne Hall; Kent and Yasemin Hamilton; Charli Hand; Mark Victor Hansen; Penny Harcum; Kristine M. Holmgren; Gayla Woolf Holt; Ruth Holton; Emily Houlik and the Houlik family; Valerie Hoybjerg; Jeanette Huber; Starr Hughes; Bob and Bobbie Hylton; Sami Kim; Elsie King; August Kund; Stephen Laudi; Paula Munier Lee; Sharon Lewis; the Lewis family; Ginny Lopez de Holien; Sandra Lovern; Rauni McDonald; Pamm McFadden; Genean McKinnon; Linda McNatt; Elisabeth McPhail; Tim Madigan; Mary Matheson; Roberta Messner; Jon and Anita Miller; Wilma Miller; the Miller family; Mindy Moore; Tonya Morrow; Debra Taylor Myers; Marie Nielsen; Amy Nihan; Ellen Patton;

Acknowledgments

Tom Lee Perry; Jenn Pfeiffer; Geanene Pickett; Louise Reardon; Rob, Carla, and Ashley Rey; Elizabeth Riley; Rosemarie Riley; Joel Roberts; Lynn Rominger; Janet Rosen; the *St. Louis Post-Dispatch*; the Sander family; Chris Stebbins; Jim and Ginger Stephens; Cynthia Stewart-Copier; Dolores Urquidi; and Marla Welch.